THE BODY, A NATION

CROATIAN IMMIGRATION DIARIES

THE BODY, A NATION

WHEN YOUR BODY IS A MEMOIR OF WAR

GARIMA SRIVASTAVA
Translated by Rajesh Kumar

Vitasta

Published by
Renu Kaul Verma
Vitasta Publishing Pvt Ltd
2/15, Ansari Road, Daryaganj
New Delhi – 110 002
info@vitastapublishing.com

First Published in Hindi in 2017

ISBN 978-93-90961-72-6

First Edition 2023
MRP 450

Translated by Rajesh Kumar
Edited by Anuradha Mukhrjee
Cover and layout by Somesh Kumar Mishra
Printed by Vikas Computer and Printers

To all those heroic women that were overcome but who finally soared to victory.

Contents

PREFACE

Journal writing is an exclusive experience, unique, almost monologic. I had never thought that these pages would see the light of day as a book, yet somehow, chronicling has turned into a habit and the wonder is that the pages even began to fill up with the accounts of quite a number of my friends and acquaintances. '*Ami hridayer katha bolite byakul, shudhailo na keho*' (I am keen to croon my feelings, but nobody wants to listen). Keenness often wilts in the absence of an audience. My family is sick of my usual tales of misery. Undeterred, I have been collecting stories here too, in Zagreb. Nadine Gordimer has termed writing a sort of suffering that demands absolute seclusion combined with self-introspection. How we delude ourselves! '*Tomar katha hetha keho to bole ne kore shudhu micche kolahal*' (Nobody talks about you here, just make a lot of noise). We must travel great distances to gather material for writing. However, no one realises the cost of these passages better than the author himself. Finally, when it is collected, he works on it alone. Roland Barthes has called writing, due to its nature, contradictory, subjective isolation, the essential link between the people amid whom we exist and the world outside. Writing is an effort for optimum articulation. Can I really deliver my best? I am uncertain because my vision turns blurry from the narratives of these women—women whose experiences were quite different from the lives of women I had known so far.

The war victims of Bosnia that I chanced upon had largely lurched out of their past; yet, for a few, the past had hardened in their lives forever, while another handful had been buried with the times gone by. When I learnt about them and met them, I found it impossible to remain indifferent or a silent bystander, the encounters also forced me to recognise myself anew as a woman. A creative artist becomes biform—you are the phenomenon and the observer. In Zagreb, as an observer, I not only gained new insight into East European society but I also found my perspective of my homeland transformed. This book contains an account of my Croatian stay and the events that followed, however, they have not been recorded chronologically. Moreover, you will not find in these pages towering protagonists of history, despite their lurking shadows. This diary is a narrative crafted by apparently insignificant affairs and bottom pickers—men, women, and children. What my interaction and sessions with them revealed do not form a part of documented history. The stories that tugged at me were neither fabricated nor fibs, I had never thought of taking them up before I moved to Zagreb.

When I ran into Dushka and Liliana, I felt their sufferings

leading me relentlessly onto distressed turf. It was a terrifying awareness. It would have been far easier for me to enjoy the natural and scenic splendour of this exotic land, to limit myself to what the government had deputed me for, but then this book would not have happened. I never realised when the sorrow of women from Eastern Europe started claiming space in my journal while I was translating *A Very Easy Death* by Simone de Beauvoir, a global feminist and explorer of women's sensibilities. Every time I tried to walk away from them, they barred my path with their mute, teary, hazel eyes. The accounts of women from Bosnia, Herzegovina, and Croatia often started me out of sleep, a continual gnawing. My only deliverance was to write the journal because nobody in India seemed even remotely interested in their tales of woe; nobody had the time to share my sense of unease. Even state-of-the-art communication technology was incapable of bridging this chasm.

The clock ticks on as we assure ourselves that these ostensibly vigorous and gorgeous women must have blanked out their grief and stepped into the mainstream—nothing can subdue the rush of life. Yet, Cathy Caruth has pertinently pointed out that devastation generates not only mental trauma but also leads to a crisis of identity. I wonder if any volume of history has offered space to these women.

A war has durable consequences. Women lose their families, some lose the trust of their close ones, and many have to peddle their bodies to eke out a livelihood. Although my family background should have made me despise sex workers, my heart—populated by characters like Nalini, Jamila, and

Vidya—overflowed with compassion and pity when I heard their stories. It is only humane to stand by these creatures who were treated with derision and viciousness by their own communities. Civilisation splits them into respectable and disreputable social orders on moral grounds. They receive only neglect and savagery; empathising with them is the true mark of humanity. Women pushed to the margin, starving, maltreated, and battered refugee kids scrounging for torn packets of potato chips, girls traded in Arizona Market like livestock, it is hard to say when they overwhelmed my consciousness. After reading certain portions of the journal, one of my friends once asked me curiously why my heart bleeds only for women on the margin; there must be some credible reason. Let me assure you, these pages were not scripted to manufacture an argument or hypothesis as it is not even systematically constructed. Its significance lies in the statement and communication of a disremembered past.

Smaller nations emerging from the disintegration of Yugoslavia, in clashes and skirmishes between 1992 and 1995, suffered great losses. Civilian peace was shattered, human rights were violated, and large-scale displacement followed, resulting in millions of people being reduced to refugees. Women bore the brunt of violence in the war because their bodies were used as sites of exploitation. It does not matter where war happens, it is ultimately the women that suffer. Still, our perspectives of violence and sexual abuse remain empty until we encounter the phenomena personally.

This evening, amid unfamiliar smells and voiceless cries,

as I transcribe the revelations by women who have disappeared from collective memory, Siada Wravich's words haunt me. 'Before I met the rape victims, I used to believe that rape was nothing but the male creature's psychopathic delinquency—an assault targeting women's genitalia, a spectacle that the press and media still call sensational, breaking news! Specious arguments are advanced e.g. the offender was incapable of self-restraint or that a particular dress aroused him or that it is man's overriding primitive instinct. Now, I realise that the trigger is not sexual thrill but fear of death. The offences are not set off by the instinct of self-defence; no man can ever claim that he retaliated sexually because the woman had attacked him. Rapes are wounds that smart terribly although the scars are invisible. It is the most powerful weapon of assault that wrecks the mind and the heart at once, a hurt so grievous that the abused, the rape victim, becomes incapable of articulating it ever fully.'

The far-reaching consequences of the Second World War had prepared the grounds for the Serb-Croat Bosnian conflict during 1939-45 when the United States of America and Soviet Russia declared Cold War against each other. Nations were divided into two camps under communist Russia and capitalist America. The possibility of a real war was never far away. The Berlin Crisis, Korean War, Russian nuclear test, Sino-India Crisis, and Cuban Missile Crisis were direct upshots of the Cold War. The East European countries joined the Soviet camp and Soviet Russia eventually set up a joint military organisation under the Warsaw Pact in 1955. Twelve nations allying with America organised themselves under the umbrella of NATO.

The international picture changed rapidly during this period. The principal cause of Soviet Union's disintegration was the lure of capitalism. The cry for democracy grew louder in several communist countries too. In such testing times, Yugoslavia did not remain immune to the democratic pressures in Poland and Romania. The emaciation of Soviet Russia accelerated the disintegration of Yugoslavia; Tito's absence catalysed it.

Today, Slobodan Milosevic is an object of loathing in Croatia, Bosnia, and Herzegovina. People construct history through their own involvement in affairs. The US-USSR relations were not a preoccupying issue for the Serbs during these times. They were smitten with Milosevic—their president in 1989. He sowed the seeds of aggressive nationalism among Serbians. My Croatian friends have told me that citizens of Serb origin suffered atrocities and torture at the hands of the Muslim majority in neighbouring Albania. When Milosevic witnessed political instability in Albania, following the collapse of the communist government, he directed the Serb people to declare Kosovo a dominion meant only for pure Serbs, free from non-Serb presence. Serb citizens accepted Milosevic naïvely as their champion without realising his overvaulting political ambitions, and what eventually followed was a concatenation of murders, arson, and pillage. The barbaric genocide can be compared only with Adolph Hitler's holocaust. In the 1990 polls, the anti-imperialist forces prevailed in Slovenia, Croatia, Bosnia-Herzegovina, and Macedonia. Slovenia and Croatia declared themselves independent. Milosevic sent in the militia to crush the insurrection, resulting in gruesome bloodshed that forced around two million people to flee as refugees.

The reports founded on the records and submissions collected by NGOs, governments, and western feminist organisations in various villages after the 1995 war are appalling yet contradictory. In the rural parts of the Zenika region in Bosnia, one rape was reported every twenty-four hours on average. It was much lesser in the towns and cities. The fact, however, is that only one out of ten cases was probably reported. The Bosnian government presented a figure of 50,000 sexually abused women; Zvonimir Separovic (who worked for the war victims) believed it was 30,000, while the European Union claimed it was only 20,000. American feminists too gathered and analysed the data on the sexually abused women in Bosnia. However, two inferences from the reports irk me—apart from the contradictory figures. The first is that rapes and sexual abuse follow a war inevitably, and second, that when the Bosnian and Croatian soldiers moved to the frontline, the women remaining behind lured the Serb soldiers to have sex. The feminists fudged the records to establish specific hypotheses in their report submitted to the UN. Enloe, Otto, and Vance were convinced that a majority of the sexual relations during the war were voluntary. They advised the women to ignore their experiences of rape and sexual abuse during the war and to move on to lead normal lives. A large number of women, disheartened by such reports, must have refrained from narrating their woes. Jesmia Husnawovic, a researcher on Bosnian and Herzegovinian women, bolstered them, 'Overlook your scars, supplant pain with joy and happiness, step into the politics of hope on the strength of your imagination, creativity and political reconstruction, and emerge before the world as political liberators'.

Innumerable tales of exploitation, violence, and torture are strewn here in the wind. They convince us that control over the woman's body is a part of the war strategy. It fulfils three objectives—one, it spreads fear; second, it drives away a population; third, rape becomes a reward for soldiers. In developing nations, the study of the issue of sexual offences against women in the backdrop of displacement and insecurity can help us understand the warp and woof of gender, sexuality, and the constructs and character of communal identity. I believe war is an industry, the incidents of which provide us with the fodder for conferences and workshops. Throughout the world, a staggering amount is spent on allocation and accommodation of the statistics of violence, killings, rape, displacement, and rehabilitation during wars. We learn about places like Srebrenica or Kigali only because they were massacre spots. Gradually, places become part of a traveller's itinerary, boosting tourism. People fascinated by the dark, neglected nooks of history use the spots for research projects; research scholars and experts arrive in hordes. The incidents connected with these locations ultimately furnish diverse indicators for art, literature, history, and sociology.

These jottings, maybe I should call it a journal, were scribbled when I was deputed at the oldest university in East Europe, Zagreb. I did not feel like publishing it for four years after I returned to India, often debating with myself what purpose it would serve. A specific mental state is required to relate to the narratives and experiences of these war victims from distant Europe. Several of the women mentioned in the pages of this journal are still my friends on Skype, they will remain my friends in the future too. Some of them found it extremely difficult to speak about themselves; some took an age to open up. Some communicated and some sealed their lips. A few refused outright; the majority spoke only on the condition of anonymity. In contrast, a few women shared their joys and sorrows so frankly that they became a part of my consciousness too.

Memories of joy, happiness, and delight fade with time but we connect intensely and ineradicably with the sufferings. When I talked to them, I realised that sharing the misery of others subsumes our personal horizons in order to enlarge our sensibilities. In fact, literature, music, and the arts instruct us on how to obliterate our self-imposed restrictions. Usually, we share our joys and sorrows only with ourselves in a personal cosmos and ignore the wide world outside—we do not care about what is happening in other parts of the nation, or in Asia or Europe. We must realise that history is not only what is printed in textbooks but also the episodes secured in legends, experiences, and racial mnemonics.

Before I left for Europe, I had read disturbing accounts of the historic Partition of India. I had gone through books, seen a couple of films, and shared the agonising memories of the victims of the 1984 anti-Sikh riots but I was a kid then, and therefore, I did not perceive the real dynamics of displacement and the refugee problem. Nowhere else in the world were so many people dislocated in such a short period. The Partition exiled 1,20,00,000 people, massacres were unleashed on unimaginable scales, and around 75,000 women fell prey to physical abuse and rape. Governments did exist in both countries, but they were incapable of delivering a dignified life and proper rehabilitation to the displaced people.

Urvashi Butalia has surmised based on the numbers of the displaced and the slain, as recorded in history books, that history is also traceable in the stories that were part of the experiences of ravaged women from both India and Pakistan. Life would not have been easy in the grim times of war and Partition—violence, large-scale displacement, the fear of being ravaged, corruption, and rehabilitation of refugees—it is hard to determine the truth in the muddle. The war continues long after the guns fall silent—dislocation, apprehensions, bigotry, racial purity, pure blood rapes and murders are not mere words for the victims, they transmute into noises that hound them during peace times too. Contexts of war vary from person to person. For a few, it is an industry but for many, it is synonymous with agony. War changes everything—human relations, love, hate, and happiness—everything acquires new connotations. The war calcifies in the memory of the victims; a mother in Sarajevo (Bosnia) finally traces her two daughters in a Foka brothel fifteen years after the war, and people keep disinterring their dead in burial fields years after the war in search of their loved ones—there are numerous such stories.

War is a complex entity—it is also a massive industry. Official statistics and books cannot cover the entire extent of its truth due to political and cultural reasons. How do we distinguish how a victim identifies resources of life during war and beyond it? What mental and corporal strategies are adopted by women to deal with the conditions during a war since their charge of small children, cattle and home care does not let them run away so easily? Displacement, rapes, economic crises, and social and familial rejection settle their future, leading to brothel conglomerates like Arizona Market in post-war periods. History is dumb on these issues—silent, soughing. It is chilling even to hear the accounts of war—war in the pages of textbooks and the war one encounters in real life are entirely different. Books do not allude to individual agonies in war. James Young believes that history texts are not the only source of information on the holocaust—our imagination is deepened also by narratives, memories, and testimonies. It is only after their perusal that we are able to fathom its dreadful nature. It is not just the facts that count, it is also important to understand how human beings, especially women, perceive it. Men and women think on different planes—Elaine Showalter has pointed out in *A Literature of Their Own* that the perspectives and experiences of men and women are disparate, they almost operate as discrete social institutions; each has its own limitations as well. Women's experiences are mostly connected with the treatment of their bodies and hence they do not think like men. They have their own constraints, defining their unique sense-appropriation and self-expression. Legitimate scrutiny of a woman's narrative—practical issues in her life, the nooks and niches of her subconscious, the fissures, hurts and anguishes, racial discrimination as well as apartheid, myriad facets of exploitation, her social temperament, gender prejudice, modalities of language adopted to assert her female identity, experiences, her posturing, tools of protest, factors behind surrender and vulnerability, physical limitations, motherhood matters, and self-contradictions—is crucial to comprehend the social interaction of women to understand these concerns.

Women were never acknowledged as a controlling force in society; power and establishment management were considered anathema to them. Patriarchal powers have always brainwashed women into believing that women themselves evade the responsibility of being a regulatory influence in society. They were always prevented from articulating themselves effectively. Carolyn G. Heilbrun has noted in *Writing a Woman's Life* that women were prohibited from becoming a part of the text, narrative, or illustration for the fear they might usurp power or for the apprehension of them growing independent of men. In fact, women express themselves more efficiently and transparently, social practices translate into an exciting experience with immediacy and totality in their narrations. A woman's experience is not chattel; it turns universal through voicing the ken of a social institution.

It is crucial to evaluate the way women remember their excruciating past because it illuminates the dark, neglected recesses of history. Memories revive continually; each revival is swayed by or blended with accretions and therefore it becomes important to ascertain how they are presented and to whom. Conventions of history intentionally reinterpret incidents, sometimes sequentially and sometimes with bias. Collective and individual elucidations, too, play a vital role in reconstructing the past.

I have collected the narratives from the memoirs of women whose present is a continuation of their past. Although their past shaped their present, yet this sort of life was not their personal choice. It was not easy either to connect with them, except those who became my close friends during my Zagreb stay—Guldane Kalin, Dushka, and Dragitsa made my life eminently bearable in this foreign land. Kresho Kernitz, Igor, and Tomislav Maretic provided me with opportunities to figure out the past and the present of Europe. Still, be it Bolkovec or Nisa, they were reluctant to speak about themselves—it was pointless, they said, to dig up the past—the chapter was closed and sealed. I encountered this contention so many times that I almost began to feel guilty. Why don't we know about them? Did we ever ponder over the fact that these apparently prosperous and happy-looking European women suffer the same fate as their Third World counterparts? Why are they averse to speaking about themselves? Unwilling to divulge their bloody past branded permanently in their psyche, does the gesture have a special significance? Are only the horrifying facts recorded in the annals central or were they in some way deeply rooted in the consciousness of the common man also? Was it something that would have precariously revealed man's inconsistent nature, his destiny and his complex inner conflicts, never documented in chronicles? It was a travesty of history, impossible to disregard when opportunism, plunder, and uncivilised animal instincts scarred the victims' hearts and minds. It was also impossible to disregard the scourge of sexually transmitted diseases and a forcibly produced generation of growing, brown-eyed teenagers. The question persists—why should a people require an exclusive history? The perpetrators were their immediate neighbours, never missing an opportunity to ransack and ravage. Ironically, they remained neighbours even after the tragedy. The master of the house, a returnee from the concentration camps with countless lesions on his mind and body—his tongue and eyes remained painfully mute. The women, who were forced into pregnancy in the absence of their husbands, and the children born from such pregnancies, were glaring testimonies of the frightful happenings during the war. Bosnians, Serbs, and Croatians suffered, but for the women whose lives turned into a combat zone, it was not so easy to relate their war woes.

If we agree with James Young, we can say that war is not only what is recorded in books but also the consequent times when people feel more at ease in forgetting it. Facts are not always the evidence, there have been innumerable debates and arguments on the issue; a person living the memory of a war generates his own individual life view. Similarly, the experiences of dislocation, exploitation, rape, and rehabilitation also are intensely individual encounters. It is not my objective to evaluate each concern through the looking glass of historiology, but can we really understand the history of a race, community, or nation if we overlook the incidents fixed in their memories of a people? I doubt it. If the narratives of these women drew me, the reasons were political as well as personal. Contemporary politics, the mad race to join the European Union, and the game of political partisanship on the one hand, and my natural propensity to think as a woman on the other—these were the factors that motivated me to take note of these unheard voices. I also learnt how religious beliefs and differences, racial identity, and ethnic purity turn so central that mass rapes and the robbing of neighbours and friends follow naturally in the wake. Besides violence, arson and plunder in war, the woman's body becomes a physical site for exploitation—her entire being is reduced to a vagina. She can be battered to avenge the stockpile of hatred, her womb can be assaulted, and she can be forced into pregnancy. The bigger tragedy is that no fulsome strategy has been formulated to render justice to these rape victims. Sometimes she is asked to furnish evidence, she is asked to present the medical certificate. In a majority of cases, women do not complain to the authorities because they do not receive support from family and community. Which memories of war are to be preferred—of terror, fear, or hatred bequeathed from generation to generation, or of the men that perpetrated the act of rape at someone else's behest but then were never able to put behind them the pitiful cries of their helpless victims? The screams of innocent girls and women hounded them into mental disorders that could not be healed even by radical nationalism. Which truth is real—the woman who went crazy after the mass rape or the woman who was forced to undress to save her infant or is it the women flotsam in the sex racket of

Arizona Market? The gap of these fifteen-odd years must have influenced their remembered narratives as every victim presents his or her version of the happening with an avowal of one's own guiltlessness. Memories are deceptive; they rise at inappropriate moments and are recumbent in repeated narratives. My endeavour is to decipher the unheard silences. They may reveal the distortions in modern man's life and thoughts—tragedies of rapes and wars in the name of aggressive nationalism. They may also suggest the necessary modification in our viewpoints of history—maybe it will take us close to reality or maybe we will glimpse some facet of the so-called, devious form of truth! Amen!

Finally, I must express gratitude to my friends whose various presences and absences gave me the courage and determination to write this journal.

(This travel journal was written during the two academic sessions of 2010-2011 at Zagreb University when I was deputed there.)

Garima Srivastava

JNU, New Delhi

TRANSLATOR'S NOTE

Is a fully resolved negotiation between languages and cultures possible ever? We pitch for equivalence, expecting that the processed product replicates the primary narrative but what actually binds this world of argots together is not merely the customary prescript of constructs in all languages but also the fact that emotions engendered from individual and shared misery are consistently ubiquitous. The translator slogs across an alchemy of languages to assume and re-inscribe joys and sorrows, ecstasies and agonies, albeit it would amount to an inflationary statement if I say that lettered simulation can approximate the mutable shades of sentiments and emotions.

However, Garima Srivastava's Hindi book, *Deh Hi Desh*, clutched my interest as a translator for this very reason of attaining a nearly impossible degree of empathy. A personal account of her stint as professor of Hindi at a Croatian university, it draws one into a disquieting journey of the sufferings of women in the war-torn European region of the former united Yugoslavia.

Women are indubitably the first spoils of war, as so poignantly suggested by the profound Hindi title of the work. How can a similar impact be brought about into the English title?, - for transliteration only appropriates the sense and may unleash the reader's imagination onto a radically altered orientation. Such dilemmas are common to translators all over the world and it is only with a degree of compromise that one is beguiled into the possibility of re-positing the sensibility of one language into another.

The Hindi work wends in an intensely experiential manner from the hinterland of Bengal at Visva-Bharati University to the dark assassinations, rape and molestation of women in the European "white region." With the doomsday clouds hovering over the horizon in this second decade of the 21st century, suggesting grimly a possible outbreak of another world war with the martial insolence of despotically ambitious tyrants, the actualities described and mentioned in the book confirm prophetically the belief that man has always used woman as a lesser language. It is exacting to transcribe instinct into words but Garima has accomplished it to a most subtle degree, identifying and visualizing, like the poet Keats who wrote in a letter to his friend Bailey in 1817, "... if a sparrow come before my window, I take part in its existence and pick about the gravel."

This translation is an agonizing descent into the sentiments of dispossession, oppression and disowning and displacement in the multiplex of tongues inhabiting the book – Hindi, Bangla, Bhojpuri, English, Croatian – a daunting inventory.

To compensate for my lexical insufficiency, I often contacted Garima to intuit what undercurrent her narrative carried at certain evasive moments and every single chance she helped me out with the greatest affability, salvaging me from the swamping fog of multivalence. Every so often my soul shivered as I battled with the peer-words that would carry across the anguish of these women - whether incarcerated by their neighbours as sex slaves or by voluntarily becoming a fleshly commodity at Arizona Market to sidestep ignominy and to sustain their families.

This translation has also been a journey of self-discovery for me.

Rajesh Kumar
Former Dean, Humanities
Vinoba Bhave University, Hazaribag

THE BODY, A NATION

THIS MAIDEN December week, the voyage from Hyderabad to Delhi and then to Zagreb appears imminent. There is a world of difference between a brief foreign trip and an extended stay abroad. My zeal has wilted in the conundrum of packing valises and the wicked midnight departure for the airport. The plane zooms on, the hours stretch interminably. I can see cottony, greyish clouds outside. The usual hubbub of the early hours of the flight has gradually been replaced by tedium and drowsiness; occasionally, droning announcements interrupt. The voice is not distinct, however, the screen in front of me reveals the plane is flying north-west after leaving Delhi, across a distance of 2342.76 nautical miles or 4338.79 kilometres over Pakistan, Afghanistan, and Kazakhstan, onward to Moscow.

There are plenty of Indians on the flight. Instead of curvaceous air hostesses on board, there are middle-aged, on-the-decline, drained looking Russian air hostesses, handing over food packets mechanically to passengers, and then dozing off in their seats. The constant trips, the clamour of passengers with their endless whinges and demands, must be exhausting and dreary. They do not flash pearly smiles like their Indian counterparts. Sometimes, I feel they are jaded housewives, fed up with the unbroken stream of guests, day in and day out. Often the plane seems to be absolutely still amid clouds; a couple of travellers are busy with their laptops, and a few converse in subdued tones. The pilot makes faint flight announcements intermittently in the most uninspiring manner as if he also knows that it is simply a chore to be performed; nobody is actually interested in listening.

What is the hour? I don't really feel like finding out the Delhi time. I have removed my wristwatch and stowed it in the laptop bag. My co-passenger is a twenty-something girl, Kalyani 'Agen'. She too is dozing off. She has finished her engineering from Hyderabad and has been trying her luck in Moscow for almost two years—she washes pots and pans in a hotel kitchen to meet her expenses. She is carrying a huge supply of curry leaves with her cabin luggage; maybe she cannot get them in Moscow. Dusky, sunburnt, clad in a salwar suit, a *bindi* adorning her forehead, she informs me she would try one more year, who knows, she might land a respectable job. How does she feel about leaving her village? She comes off with a whole account of Peddapuram, her native place—there is still no electricity in her village, located on the Godavari Delta. A few men practise agriculture but most of the families sustain themselves through the earnings of their daughters. Uneducated girls take up prostitution to maintain their destitute dependents. In most families, at least one daughter is a sex worker. They belong to the sub-caste Kalavanthalu, where singing and dancing is their traditional occupation. Kalyani has somehow managed her education by mortgaging her land. She secured a 15K job in Hyderabad but it was insufficient, so she finally shifted to Moscow. Even small jobs here enable her to send 25,000 a month back home.

What time is it? The Moscow clock must be around three hours behind. The left half of my back has stiffened from sitting so long. The plane lands and a white blanket covers everything. The thick carpet of snow at Shermetyov airport is dazzling. The large wings of the plane are being de-iced incessantly with hot water sprays. The brightness of the snow and its spread is almost frightening. Commuters deplane with their luggage. Kalyani has melted into the crowd after sharing her email. The real challenge faces me now—numerous terminals and the long distances between them have to be covered on foot. In the lengthy waiting queues, everyone speaks only Russian; the languages I know are useless here. And these stringent security checks at every turn! Your word is not enough.

I have to catch another flight for Zagreb, but I am lost between terminals. My excitement for the Europe tour is on the wane although I have just begun. T.S. Eliot once asked, 'Do I disturb the universe?' I am in a similar predicament.

How does it matter whether I write or not? Hundreds in this world have jotted down the sagas of their experiences, joys and sorrows, feats and their fights, their likes and dislikes and then passed away unnoticed. They did not know who their readers were. Did their writing light a path for someone? Did it inspire anyone? Still, experiences must be shared, despite the impossibility of organising and retaining them. Isn't it a fact that their advent too is equally chaotic?

***

It is February now. I have not written a single word, let alone chronicled the events. A month and a half have passed in this quaint little town, Zagreb, by the Adriatic in mid-south Europe. Some of my friends and associates believe Croatia is in Asia. Many of them tried to dissuade me—why would you travel to Europe in such frigid weather? Should I disclose that my thirst to walk the world has drawn me to this place? When I was a kid, I could barely control my excitement whenever I saw my elder sister, four years older, leaving for school in her uniform and shoes, lugging her satchel. Mother put me in school when I was just around two and a half. The shoes, however, proved literally too big for me, incarcerating me swiftly into the harsh regimen of the seminary. I never really enjoyed a true childhood.

***

The Indian Council for Cultural Relations has expressed its intentions to set up a Department of Hindi at Zagreb University and I am lucky enough to be selected for the assignment. The job is to be finished in two years. The students here are eager. I enjoy the short two-kilometre walk from the guest house to the university. Transport and communication facilities are excellent; the entirety of Croatia is interconnected by eight national highways. The university is in Ivana Yelachica, while the Indian embassy is located in downtown Kulmerska. Thankfully, I do not have to visit the embassy regularly. The Indian Ambassador, Mr Pradeep Kumar, is polite but a disciplinarian; most often he is on tours back to India. The Second Secretary looks after the embassy. The employees and the officials are all decent, Mrs Pasi and Aryan; I love talking with them in Hindi. The three-storeyed white building is spotless and well-kept, but life seems wooden here.

I have requested the Head of the Indology Department, Prof Yeric Mislav, to find a house for me close to the university. The embassy runs in a leased bungalow; there is a thick, orderly woodland behind it. There are staircases and a profusion of blossoms and blooms, mostly olive trees. My family and friends back in India are quite curious about this place. There are rows of residential houses half a kilometre up the boulevard, on the right flank of Viesnik Tram Station. I have been requested to stay in the fifth-floor flat of Elvira Mestrovic on cvjetni-cesta (Flower Street). It is a lovely flat, snug. The front is open and airy. Elvira Mestrovic stays in Germany, she is a woman of taste and sophistication, and the house is a living testimony.

Zagreb University has leased it for me; the accommodation is more than ample. It sports an open kitchen and there are two fridges. The embassy has sent in my stuff. Everything I have brought from India has been tidied up. The laptop is my prized possession because it is going to be my steady companion now.

Although it is February, the weather is rather weird. The temperature hovers at four to six degrees below zero. The sun shines sporadically for brief spells. I shiver even when the sun is out. Snowstorms gust now and then, without warning. Inside the house, it is pretty comfortable; it is air conditioned, warm, but I do not get the urge to peer outside the window.

It is a Sunday. My watch still shows Delhi time. Here it is four and a half hours behind. I have already eaten breakfast. Oats and fruit curd. I feel like taking a nap. I dream I am in my own country, now with my siblings, now with Manjudi in Santiniketan. We are in the Ratanpalli house, making fun of Chaitalidi's staunch, unwavering faith in Sai Baba. When the milk boils over in the pan, she blows on it, chanting '*Jai Sai*'. When I tell her she should switch off the gas oven, that no Sai Baba would materialise here to turn the knob, she gets riled. Ma is frying *pua* in Delhi on Holi. She stirs vigorously the white flour, milk, sugar, and dry fruits and then drops the batter dollops in sizzling clarified butter like a master chef. With a sputter, the *pua* blossoms into shape. She prepares the jackfruit *salan* in *garam masala* (spices), followed by *littis*. Nobody can beat Dadi in cookery. The crisp *litti*, overstuffed with gram flour, garlic, and bishop's weed, served with mouth-watering spicy eggplant mash. And the flavour, rare even to gods, men, and sages! The delicacies dance before me with all their irresistible spread, aroma, and essence. Manjudi used to prepare pea *kachauris* in Shantiniketan. The savoury semolina *halwa* cooked by Harishchandraji on Gandhiji's death anniversary, the taste lingers. I wake up with a start, breathing hoarsely. The room is pitch-dark, empty. Am I here or not?

> *Kabe kee hai hawaas kabhi ku-e-butan kee hai*
> *Mujhko khabar nahin meri mitti kahan kee hai.*
> (Now I yearn for the Kaba, now for the street of idols,
> Know not I, where I truly belong.)
>
> —Dagh Dchalvi

What place is this? Has my elder sister, preparing for the medical entrance exam, switched on the lights? She sleeps during daylight hours and studies whole nights. She calls out—Soni, if you keep sleeping, when will you study? Where is Ukki? Must be playing with dolls below the overturned wooden stool with her friends under the guava tree. See, she is wearing her slippers wrong again, she is little but so independent-minded, so aware—she never shares the bed with anyone in the family. Not even after Mom's death, not even with Bua. She has conjured her own private world at the young age of four. Should I put on the slippers? Should I get up? Friends from Hindu College have come down to invite me—two of our teachers—Dr Harish Naval and Suresh Rituparna have asked us to their house. After the party, I return with Smitadi in the evening. Rameshwarji 'Ajneya' teaches the class gravely in his baritone voice. What if he asks questions in the session tomorrow? The end is near! It is the class of Dr Krishna Dutt Paliwal. Nikilesh Jha is my senior—he is mimicking Paliwal's smoking; we all flip. Nobody realises when he appears at the door. The finest teacher in the college, with his infallible memory, has prophesied like the angry sage Durvasa, 'You will never get anywhere in life…ever!'

What place is this? It is years back…I turn in bed with effort but my lids are leaden. I can hear the stuttering sound of gunfire in Tons valley. My first job. I am supposed to teach gentlemen cadets aspiring to become officers in the Indian Military Academy. The morning siren hoots. Exiting the barracks, I am walking in the quarter-to-6-am gloom on the damp road leading to the Army Cadet College Wing. Lampposts on the flanks glimmer. Raindrops are glued to the lampposts. Cadets march in unison, saluting me, moving on. Knot after knot passes by… where am I? The bell rings raucously. I finally get up and open the door. Kresho Kernitz looks at my dumbfounded expression and shakes my hand. His grasp carries the comforting warmth of companionship. He teaches Sanskrit at Zagreb University on a contractual appointment. Icy wind blasts in through the open door, dragging me into wakefulness. Kresho recognises my bantam anxieties. He installs Skype and Whype on my laptop to talk to India. It is only three in the afternoon but darkness has gathered. A large raven-like bird has alighted on the lamppost. There are solitary figures in the street, wrapped in overcoats. I am in Zagreb and I have to stay here for the next two years. I brood—two years is such a long time.

***

I am writing letters regularly to my friends because the weather is hazy all the time. I find it hard to guess what degree and nature of cold will accost me outside. I cannot stand the vegetarian meal served in the canteen. People here are fond of Indian food. They tell me that someone had started an Indian joint in Turkebana Yelachica (downtown Zagreb) but it finally shut shop. Boishali Ghosh is fascinated by European trivia; we are pretty good friends. She studied in Kala Bhavan at Santiniketan, I have taught there for eight long years. Boishali says, '*Tumi sab kichhu bhule shudhu ananda karo*' (forget everything, just enjoy yourself), but her advice has fallen on deaf ears. I wrote an email to Boishali on 5 February 2010.

> Dear Friend,
>
> I am sorry for the delay in sending the details of the place. My plane landed here on a snowy evening. There were strange faces all around. Professor Mislav, Head of Indology, and officials from the embassy had come down to the airport. The Zagreb airport is not large; most of the folks were dressed in black—black jackets and black shoes. My heart sank. Unfamiliar faces, pallid, vacant, freckled, Romanesque features; brown, blue, and green eyes. Alas, had someone begged me to cancel the trip saying I was not needed here, I should return! Back home, my students in their wooden chairs, familiar and intimate, must be waiting for my research methodology class. A pet does not accept food from a stranger. What is so important here? What heartache has prompted me to this strange country where only solitary

figures walk the roads? Not a soul seems bothered about me. No ants, no mosquitoes, no wasps, no hornet, no mud-wasp, no squirrel, no mynah, no woodpecker—nothing. No green neem tree swaying gaily outside the window. Had you been here, you would have told me to step outside myself, to live in the moment. I am trying my best yet I don't relish it.

You have asked about food. I do the cooking myself; the day brightens up a bit with these chores. The kitchen is filled with cooking gadgets. Croatia is renowned throughout Europe for its non-vegetarian cuisine. Freshwater fish, beef, pork, and vegetables cooked Mediterranean style are the specialities. In the cold season, large chunks of animal flesh are hung on iron hooks. The meat seasons in the smoke of burning wood in closed rooms. The smoke layer is a preservative—smoked meat. The recipe is an ancient one, pretty popular. Olive oil is a great favourite here.

The doors in the cvjetni-cesta, the alley where I live, are large and wide. Main doors carry deadbolts. Since I am new, I was locked outside my flat twice. In the flat opposite mine is Dragitsa. She does not know English, I do not know Croatian. She has spent quite some time in Italy. She speaks German and Italian. This young woman of seventy has bought a Croatian-English dictionary. Yes, she is young at heart because she is totally stress-free at this juncture of her life. A round, charming face, an aquiline nose, and trimmed blonde hair. She always looks busy, tending to the flower plants on the front terrace of her flat.

You too had planted a lot of flowers and saplings outside your house in Hyderabad. From my window they looked like islands of greenery, still, they suffered from neglect when you left. Nobody else after you was as attached to them as you were. I too moved out after a few days. When I look at Dragitsa, I imagine it is you, kneeling and weeding, in similar-looking loose pyjamas.

Don't be so anxious, my Micky Mouse! I would write again.

Bhalo theko. (Keep well)

Garima.

***

There are thirty flats in this building in cvjetni-cesta. The fifth floor flat of Dragitsa fills with life every weekend when her daughter Tanya and granddaughter Nadia visit her. Tanya is a chirpy girl, smartly turned out. She has short hair and driving is her passion. Dragitsa's thirty-five-year-old son Igor is an artist. Unemployment has made him bitter and dejected. Dragitsa has a spare key to the flat; she says Igor's erratic hours do not bother her much. Yet, her eyes reveal another story. This is the West—parents treat their children as friends when they turn seventeen. I can see the gap diminishing day by day. Nadia is so stressed by the pressure of passing her exam that she is unable to quit smoking. She does not know what she will do if she fails. She says, 'You people believe that only grown-ups are hassled. I don't enjoy my studies or staying at home. I want to grow up quickly and work as a music director or in films'. Her mother Tanya is worried sick about her. She is a technical assistant in the radiology department at the government hospital in Dubrava. She has divorced twice and is now in a relationship with a fellow called Mladen, from Rijeka, but she is always shaky about her boyfriend. She is sure if she stays away from Mladen for long periods he would stray to satiate his physical and emotional needs. When I ask her, she replies, 'You can't trust men. They are straight only as long as they get no opportunity. You relax your grip and he slips away'. Hey, it is how an Indian woman thinks! Tanya checks her boyfriend's cell phone, wallet, and emails to find a sign of betrayal.

This obsessive mistrust is risky. Exactly the sort of thing that made Dr Rao suffer a heart stroke in his Hyderabad lab. He succumbed eventually. His wife had started snooping and sniffing in the lab; it proved fatal for Mr Rao. It is only the true and the honest that the world looks up to. Had he survived, he would have earned quite a name from his discoveries. His funeral procession, two innocent kids and the stony, blank face of his wife, still inhabit my memories. Perhaps he would not have died if his wife had trusted him, because she later confessed that she did the sniffing without any ground for suspicion, simply to prevent him from falling into the honey trap of some comely research scholar. Suspicion looms over life, possession eclipses love, mistrust smothers relationships and morality distends larger than the heart—Is this the reality?

Do we realise that relationships require space like the roots of a plant? If there is no room, it dwarfs into a pitiful, diminutive bonsai. However, Tanya does not seem to have learnt any lessons from her two broken marriages.

She visits Rijeka every Friday. Her daughter Nadia too keeps out whole nights. Tanya says, 'I don't want my daughter to repeat the mistakes I made. Your country is much better because parents exercise strict control over their children'. She is wary of scolding Nadia. Tanya's mother Dragitsa is always occupied—embroidery, reading books, shopping, or gardening. Dragitsa was a nurse her whole life; she had purchased the flat with her savings. Her soldier husband died years ago. Her in-laws are in Budapest, she spends her vacations there.

***

For the last two weeks, Tanya has started visiting me on Saturdays; she adores sweet *sonpapadi*. We simply gossip. On the second Saturday in mid-February we go on a long drive by the sea. The right-hand driving seems pretty weird to me, I do not possess an international license.

Tanya opens up. She likes talking in English. Very often, as she struggles to find the English equivalent of a Croatian word, the conversation is interrupted. There are lavender bushes along the coast. The plants are around two-and-a-half feet tall. The fragrance of lavender blends with the scent of the sea, turning the entirety of South Europe humid. In France, lavender is also used in certain recipes. The fragrant, antiseptic lavender is used as a medicine for sleep disorders in Croatia and several other parts of Europe. Croatia is also distinguished for tourism and its wines. Tanya seeks my nod to drink as she describes its famous beverages. Her throat is dry.

Spread across 641.355 square miles, Zagreb is the cultural and administrative nerve centre of Croatia. In the old days, it was a Roman settlement. Hungary annexed it in 1200 AD. The Pope founded a church in Zagreb for the first time in 1094 and named it Zagreb. It is called 'Agram' in German. The history of Zagreb and Croatia is a history of hostilities. Until 1991, it was a part of Yugoslavia. It holds innumerable, quiescent stories of battles. Its frontiers are bounded by Slovenia, Hungary, Serbia, Bosnia, Herzegovina, and Montenegro. Today's Croatia, truncated to a mere 21,851 square miles, has lost one-third of its land in the conflicts. On 15 February 1992, the European Economic Community and the United Nations recognised it as a republic. For three long years until 1 August 1995, it went to war with Serbia to reclaim its land. It was granted membership in the European Union recently, on 1 July 2013. I did not have to travel far to seek the signs of the protracted campaigns. When I received permission to visit Italy and France, the Indian Embassy handed me the address of Dushanka Samrajideva's tourism company. By a stroke of luck, I discovered that Dushanka's flat is in the building where I stay.

***

I received Aninditadi's email after a very long time. She

sounded quite excited when she heard I was coming to Zagreb. She wants me to visit Europe. I type a reply on the computer:

Dear Aninditadi,

How are you?

It has taken me some time to settle down in Zagreb. You had asked me about the status of women in Europe. At present I am grappling with the hurdle of language; most people use only Croatian. The new generation does use English so I don't face any problems in class. But I must learn the rudiments of Croatian if I really want to communicate. I often recall what you had told me. Once again it is Basant Panchami. Last Basant Panchami I was at your house and we had worshipped Goddess Saraswati together.

I called you last night on Skype. Your voice was faint; I could hardly make it out. Do you never talk to anyone in the presence of your mother-in-law? I'll let you know, I find it funny to see you so tradition-bound—you, an intellectual, professor, and poet! You have always carried the millstone of relationships. Will you never break free? An extended family does not give much space to a woman to let her flourish. My conviction has grown stronger after I met your folks. Your mother-in-law was a modern and well-educated woman of her times; I can't say how much freedom she enjoyed—little or not at all. She chose you for her son but her attitude was not proper. I see old women like her here also—they are always smartly turned out, with a spring in their step. My neighbour, for example, believes in 'sixty is naughty'. What is past is over; one begins to live their life on one's own terms when the responsibilities end. We have a different mindset in our country. All the vivid tints of life are snatched away in old age. Retirement implies you don't have a right to a life of your own. Your dependence on others increases, your expectations, too, grow. Since we don't have much to occupy ourselves, we start interfering in others' lives. We start invading the spaces of others and this is the primary cause of tension in our families. Women here know how to respect this space—naturally, they do not expect much from others. I like this approach. You had told me that your mother-in-law wanted a traditional daughter-in-law, one who would be skilled at household chores—imagine, Di, the education of women is sopped up by the in-laws. It is expected that they would not choose their creativity over their duty to the family. What is the use of studies if the family is served a cold meal or if women traipse around with their *jholas*? The paradox is that women themselves act as agents of male members in this patriarchal realm. When will they realise that they have continuously been losing opportunities for enterprising accomplishments? Opportunities of writing and publishing—to secure their identity as an individual. If their daughters and daughters-in-law are creative, if they do not support them, they should not inhibit them either—not dishearten them, or shackle them.

India did not have to tackle a world war on its own but it is strange that most Indian women keep contending their individual battles on the family front. I have made a friend here, Dushanka—everyone calls her Dushka. Her life is a living testimony of the Serb-Croat war. I had read somewhere that wherever war is fought, it is the women that are the actual sufferers. War has converted Dushka's life into a constant battle. In the war, Serbs killed Croatians and burnt down their houses. In retaliation, the Croatians launched a mission to annihilate all Serbs in Croatia. Many were killed; a few escaped. Dushka's parents were unable to reach their daughters in Belgrade. Dushka was fired from her job without notice. They were reduced to mere Serbs, humans no more. The neighbours looked daggers at them. The war raged. Only one nation profited from this war—America. It claimed it was trying to bring about a truce but it went on supplying lethal arms and weapons clandestinely. No sooner was a ceasefire declared than it was broken. Zagreb was peaceful because it was the national capital. Still, it was impossible to remove hostility and hatred from the minds and hearts of the people. Croatians swore at Serbs in trams and buses and spat at them, exhibiting their hatred in every manner possible. Dushka had planned to start her own tourist agency but the war changed everything. Many men turned into millionaires overnight, many were reduced to abject penury. She received two reports simultaneously—first that the war was over and second, that she was pregnant. She ran from pillar to post, from Savski Most to Preko, she walked up to Tresnjevka but no doctor was willing to handle a Serbian girl's case. Her Croatian lover refused to recognise her; he rained insults on her, calling her a filthy Serb, not even deigning to talk to her. Dushka became an unmarried mother because the doctor told her, '*Ovo maa jadyaye vlakh*' (this is your last train). Since then she has been taking pretty good care of her parents and the son, Dino.

Dushka is an affable soul; I feel we will get on well despite the age difference. She stays in my building and we meet every Sunday. She finds it difficult to pronounce Garima so she calls me Garry. In our India, '*gair*' does mean 'stranger'—that is I.

Rest awhile.

I miss your *halwa* garnished with cardamom. Do write.

Yours,

Garima

***

Ivana, Mirta, Valentina, and Bozac often drop in. However, during weekends when an icy stillness prevails everywhere, none of them picks up my calls. I find it weird that these folks retract into their shells every weekend. Preparations for the weekend begin on Thursday night itself. Zagreb girls are more liberated than their Indian counterparts. The young generation is on the move all the time because jobs are scarce. This is the Europe of economic depression. Multinational companies announce their presence boldly with billboards—McDonald's, Reebok, Van Heusen, Adidas. Students turn into shop hands on the weekend. Paid around twenty-five to thirty kunas an hour, they are almost worked to death. My brilliant student, Carmen Vugrin, cleans and mops or washes plates and cooks in McDonald's during the weekend or summer holidays. Mariana, whose godparent at home is merely a pear tree, wears dozens of rings on her nose and ears, colourful ribbons in her hairdo, and plays her guitar in the streets and alleys of Dubrava and Turkebana Yelachica. She also strums a couple of Indian songs. She plucks strings; pedestrians fling coins on the scarf laid before her. Andriana and Bozac put on costumes and funny noses to entertain tourists. Bozac is disconcerted to see me in Turkebana. Embarrassed, he melts away into the streets.

Croatians are distinguished by their Roman features, fair complexion, towering and robust physique, and majestic gait. European prosperity makes us Indians feel inferior. Still, I see here plenty of souks but no customers. Large stores, most of them selling leather footwear, are deserted—goods fill the shelves in festooned shops but there are more window shoppers than buyers. Obviously, people's purchasing power has declined considerably. Students wait eagerly for the sale season. They buy and use old clothes dotingly. A second-hand goods market is held on the outskirts of Zagreb, along the rail route running east. It reminds me of the bazaar behind the Red Fort. Clothes, bags, shoes, belts, bed sheets, pillow covers, and belongings of dead men are sold here. One can find shirts in pretty good shape for hardly five kunas. There are lots of buyers in this market. Their favourite colours are black, white, and sable, especially in the winters that stretch for seven to eight months.

The train is a comparatively cheap and safe transport in Europe. Zagreb lies by Slovenia but one must get a Schengen visa to go there. I have already submitted my application to the embassy. Tanya will accompany me to Slovenia but first I must go to Rijeka where the Croatian translation of Rabindranath Tagore's play *Chitra* has been brought out by Cresho Karnitz and his wife Sasha's publication house. Cresho is quite a common name here. It is the shortened form of a former king, Kreshimir.

***

It is the last week of February. It is sunny outside. The snow that fell last night appears like cotton tufts by the roads. There is a sharp nip in the wind instead of softness; it is frosty. The wind shakes the snow piled on the pine branches lovingly but does not chuck it, before blowing out to the Adriatic. The cherry and fig trees have shed all their leaves. The prematurely aged stunts are enclosed effusively in snow. The trees by the road ahead of our cvjetni-cesta appear comatose in the blooming sun. Snow entices us with its soothing, hypnotic whiteness until we confront it bodily. Riding our soulful romantic dreams, visualising ourselves in snow boots and jackets, we slide down its pearly inclines with gay abandon, but when it begins to torment you night and day, drives the birds and fowls away, its magic changes into stillness in a flash. I am speechless as I peer through the window curtains of my fifth-storey flat. It is a staggering, uninterrupted whiteness. The cars in the parking below have merged into a single hoariness. A lone figure is removing the snow with a spade. He scrapes and lobs it on the flanks, near the grate of the underground drain. The piles grow. The lower road is iced but the sun is not warm enough to melt it; already it is afternoon. Garbage cans fitted with iron wheels are placed at the back of the cvjetni-cesta and all multi-storeyed buildings. The city corporation collects taxes from the citizens to maintain civic facilities. It is done with utmost sincerity, something which we miss sorely in India. Early morning, the previous day's trash collected in the bins is emptied into large trucks. The empty containers wait to be filled up again. They carry instructions in Croatian for the segregation of dry and wet waste.

***

Classes begin at the university at eight in the morning. Professor Yeric had told me that I could engage in my classes either at eight in the morning or eight in the evening. Getting into a class at eight in the evening sounds strange to me. To lecture a class after the day's exhaustion, *ow*! In India, I have always taught in the morning sessions only. By noon my energy wanes. In Santiniketan, the classes used to commence right after the *baitalik* prayers, at half past six, and I was free by one in the afternoon. The latter half of the day belonged to me. Reading, visiting the library, Kankalitala, the bridge over River Ajay, Khowai, Amar Kutir, Banalakshmi and back home by the evening—the leisure was a blessing. In Indian universities, especially in humanities and social sciences, classes finish usually by six in the evening. The sun sets, the teacher goes on a binge and the student on the fringe.

Routines embed themselves in one's life as values. Studying late hours and rising early to teach, it delights you with the anticipation of another beautiful day. Dawn endows upon you fresh energy and flair. It has prompted me to prefer the morning slot in Zagreb. A ninety-minute class followed by a break and later, another class. Usually, I return to my flat by half past one in the afternoon. Evenings are normally spent in the library. I read till late. The library is very well organised. Books in English, Croatian (Hrvatski), and French in blue and red covers—an all-embracing world of delightful volumes. Books let us absorb all the experiences that one cannot harvest in one life span. The plateaux rising in their pages, sandy oceans, dried up rivers—all these begin to dwell in us; our childhood sports, the fairy tales, are all drafted in them, and the perfume of language turns so intimate that every turn of a page, every bookmark, spawns whole new worlds. The library is air-conditioned—20° C to 22° C—a relaxed, reassuring atmosphere; nothing can compare with this ambience. Many students work on an hourly basis under the 'Earn while You Learn' scheme. They prepare catalogues, dust the books, and earn adequate pocket money. Darya is in the second year, she is bald but beautiful—I often see her busy with chores in the library. The library is as old as Sveucilista u Zagrebu, one of the oldest universities in mid-south Europe, established in 1669. Situated on the tenth street in Ivana Ulichica, this spot is my haven. Clouds veil the soft sun rays without warning, turning the day into twilight; the icy rain drizzles on, hushed. A lull everywhere, trees and shrubs lie quietly under the spotless, silvery blanket of snow, fusing the day into night. I meet Sergei Mikhailovic here; he is a polyglot, a walking encyclopedia. Retired from service but working in the library, he understands my problems.

***

I am rereading Simone de Beauvoir. Sometimes it intensifies my disquiet about being away from home and sometimes it calms me down. Reading her novels and autobiography is like going through a gratifying tragedy. The snug warmth in the library and Simone's books hold me back from returning to the reticence of my flat. I have begun to like the scent of roasted coffee beans in the air; I have also started noticing the curious babble in the coffee house. Sometimes I imagine Simone in a China crepe frock, writing at one of the tables, engrossed, her head bent in the thick of smoke rings. At Sergei's behest, I have started translating her autobiographical novel *A Very Easy Death* into Hindi. Reading Simone's works is like passing through a world of wisdom, the fountainhead of feminist theory and politics. While *The Second Sex* examines human freedom and the causes of a woman's subjugation in a patriarchal community, books like *A Very Easy Death*, *Prime of Life*, and *All Said and Done* evaluate practical aspects of feminism. Simone finished *A Very Easy Death* in 1964; it was published a year after her mother's passing away. The conversations between Simone and Maman on her deathbed in her last six weeks are an autobiographical account of profound intimacy, regrets, and moments of grief. The book traverses several peaks of role trading between the mother and the daughter, a woman's part in persecution, the bonds between husband and wife, the relationship between a doctor and a patient, and squabbles in a hospital. Maman has been a lonely widow for twenty-four years. Simone is occupied with freelance writing and her life. Maman does not realise till her last moments that she is suffering from a fatal cancer. She is not ready to die. She wants to get well and live her life anew although she is seventy-eight. Sometimes, the act of reading Simone and translating her ushers in deep loneliness within me. Now and then dim, dark shadows walk inside me; sometimes it is Simone who guides my hand as I write. I have spoken to Nityanand Tiwaryji and sent certain portions of the translation to him. He has liked it a lot but he advises me to steer clear of creative depression.

***

This evening, I take the shortcut at the back to reach cvjetni-cesta. It is twilight; in a short while the streetlights will come on. The wind is wet and gusty. The sky seems to be bearing down on me. It may rain tonight. I find it difficult to walk fast in my snow boots, the overcoat and the layers of sweaters weigh me down. There is a *mali ducan* (small store) on the way. Its glass doors are shut. The girl at the counter has reddish hair. Perhaps she has coloured it burgundy. A cigarette smoulders between her fair, slender fingers with red painted nails. I am the only customer in the store. She flings a formal smile at me with the greeting of '*Dobardaan*' (good afternoon). It is a small store selling vegetables, bread, and wine. I need to buy brown chocolate. I have read somewhere that chocolate is a mood elevator. The girl does not know English. I have selected fruit curd, red wine, and chocolates in the plastic tray. She calculates the bill on her computer and takes my card. I have learnt to say '*Khvala*' (thanks).

This week I have called Dushka home but an invitation without wine is like food without salt. I quicken my steps and soon I am at the back of my house. Silence reigns all around. A pale pool of light filters from the white curtains of the nearby flat. Something is astir near the garbage bins. Inquisitively, I glance in that direction. A woman in a long, frock-like coat and black boots—whom I have often noticed walking into the flat across ours—is almost half hanging in the bin, scouring for dry trash. I am in the shadows behind the fig tree. This lady in high-heeled boots and a cocked hat in the daytime, who marched haughtily with a dog on a leash, what is she doing in the garbage bin at dusk? I am curious. In a short while, her gloved hands draw out and dump used shoes, old clothes, umbrellas, and pots and pans in a large polythene bag placed on the ground. The woman half hanging in the bin emerges. Cautiously, holding her breath and trying to suppress the crackle of the plastic bag, she lifts it. It is large, probably heavy too, but she somehow braces herself and moves towards her flat with practised steps.

***

These days I often get out for a walk in the evening. A few old people are sitting on the benches in the park. Elderly people receive a nominal government pension as well as an unemployment allowance but the taxes are so stiff that it is not of much help. Dragitsa evades the subject with a smile. Croatians are a proud people, they dislike talking about a neighbour to a foreigner.

It is flower season in Croatia. Zagreb University is famous for growing three varieties—highland flowers, seasonal ones, and marsh blossoms. They are pretty costly in the market but the horticulture department cultivates around 5,500 types. Some of them look familiar. Besides the numerous varieties of roses, there are nora barlow, rudbekia, varieties of iris, vanilla planifolia, euphorbia milii, nuphar lutea, mistosis ultra marine—flowers I have seen for the first time. These gorgeous, serene, hardy florets blossom and wither away to play their transient life cycle; however, we believe our life and world shall never cease.

***

The climate in India never confined me within the walls of my house. To spend an indoor life willingly and to be circumscribed under duress—the two situations are vastly apart. In the latter, your spirit roams outside although the body is detained. Sometimes you press your nose against the window pane to gaze at the drizzle, sometimes you stare at the frozen Sawa River and imagine the water flowing beneath. Cars zoom over the Sawa Bridge. People have taken their pets to the parks for a stroll. Solitary figures sit on benches. A dog training session is on in one corner of the park, there are various breeds. Their training and grooming are noteworthy. People are very particular that their pets should not pester anyone; fines are hefty.

India too has its share of dog lovers. One of the professors at Hyderabad University is so fond of canines that every night he throws banquets for them in front of his residence. The mongrels on the campus invite their friends around vociferously. Sometimes, the food is not enough for all of them and the deprived ones growl like the proletariat barking at the bourgeoisie. The curs transform into lions after the hearty meal, and the ear-splitting canine concerto commences and resonates till midnight. The barks inside inspire the dogs outside the campus to demonstrate their woofing skills. The dog-lover professor snores in bed with the contented feeling of '*sarve bhawantu sukhinah*' (let all be happy) and his neighbours wait for the concerto to conclude because if you try to drive away the dogs, you will invite the ire of the Menka Gandhi animal loving squad. Fondness for dogs is also a mark of sophistication among the residents on the campus. One of the women professors loves them so dearly that she would stop anywhere to coddle them. In these times of social aloofness, maybe such behaviour forms a part of 'practical interaction', an excuse for ignoring one's acquaintances. Some of the men-folk would certainly love to be dogs in such a state of affairs, maybe!

***

I have not been keeping well almost for a week. The doctor to whose clinic I was sent by the embassy knows only how to add up an enormous bill, besides flashing smiles, so I opt for the main hospital at Dubrava. Tanya works here. It is multistoried, spick and span, and the doctors and nurses are prompt. Shops on its perimeter sell lovely wares. It is quite unhospital-like on the campus. There is no confusion that one encounters in Indian hospitals. Benches are laid out in the open. There are flower beds and creepers, and the wind carries the scent of lavender leaves. I have already spent seven days in the hospital. Doctor Marinovic is a thoracic specialist. He informs me my swollen tonsils have caused the fever. I enjoy strolling in the hospital whenever my fever is down. Tanya's office is in another section of the building. Although she seldom has free hours, we do manage to meet. There is a seventy-five-year-old, graceful-looking woman in the bed beside mine. She keeps waiting for someone all the time, I have sensed it in the last four or five days. She does not sleep, sobbing whole nights. She does not speak to me. She has had surgery; plastic tubes and bags dangle from her belly, filling slowly with blood. The nurse tells me that she comes from a prosperous family but nobody visits her. The nurses are Italian and German, stout and attentive, they perform their duty mechanically. There are male nurses too in the women's ward; there is no gender discrimination in healthcare. The Croatian nurses are cheerful, frank, and gregarious, one can often see them gossiping at the nursing station. Cured patients place flowers and chocolates on the counter. Doctors wear green, nurses are in white and pink. Creepers bearing white flowers fill the space outside the window.

Guldane often stops by; she has taken three days' leave from the university. I had never imagined somebody would become so close to me in a foreign land. We often sit on the benches in the sun, talking and filling our nostrils with the lavender-scented, cold, saline air that will eventually blow out to my native country. I feel dejected when Guldane misses a visit. I have made several rounds of the hospital. The members of the staff have grown familiar with my face but my eyes well up as I swallow the bland soup and the apple pie. Although there is an assortment of dishes on the hospital menu, I cannot eat ham and sausages. The beef and chicken soup rise like a stink to me. There *are* bananas and apples but they do not satisfy my hunger. I wish somebody would ask me lovingly how I am faring—would I prefer rice and lentils? Or maybe mango pickles and *khichadi*, *moong khichadi* with pure *ghee* poured over it, or else fresh *rotis* baked on the griddle with *tadka* lentils. But then, there is nobody here, nobody will bring me anything. Does an illness make us ache for our loved ones? When you fall sick, you yearn for somebody to be at your bedside, caring, expecting you to recover quickly. Oh Lord, I don't ever want to fall sick again!

***

My hospital stint is over. The stay in the hospital was also a journey through *A Very Easy Death*, which lent me new insight into the bonds between Simone and her mother. Simone's novels, *She Came to Stay* and *The Mandarin*, have helped me appreciate the feminist countenance in these postmodern times. The reading of her autobiographical novels has been a gripping and scrupulous rendezvous. My illness and convalescence in the hospital have brought me closer to Simone. She compares herself with Sartre during her time as a scholar in the university and her keenness to 'think like a man' in *Memoirs of a Dutiful Daughter* finally brings her to the conclusion that it is improbable for a woman to think like a man. In *Prime of Life,* Simone talks about her stay in hotels for her studies—her continual hops from one boarding house to another. I wonder how Simone met her expenses; moreover, if you stay in a hotel, you are simply a passing guest. The bed, curtains, the chair and the table, you own nothing.

While reading Simone, the reader learns how to pass one's time in the cafeteria, how to see people, how to study, and how to assume and argue. Simone suggests that if you walk into a cafeteria and suddenly espy two close friends of yours lost in talk, you must not interrupt them. It is better to move away to some other seat. Simone believes that a coffee house can be a space for studies and recounts how she went on long walks during the years she taught in small towns like Marseilles and Rouen in the 1930s, without expecting anyone to accompany her. I suppose it is difficult for a woman to obtain a space of her own even today. In India, if a woman is discovered alone in a coffee house and writing, umpteen pairs of eyes would begin to disapprove.

I am feeling better now, going through *Force of Circumstances*, the volume in which Simone de Beauvoir portrays post-war Paris. It envisions a new, superior society. It introduces a sense of duty to the concept of freedom. She has mentioned her relationship with Nelson Algren in this section of her autobiography. She has also related having sex with Nelson in front of the fireplace and their individual lives in Paris and Chicago. Geographical distances have a tendency to smother even the most intimate relationship. She writes that she did not leave Paris because writing was her passion. She has also given an account of her long journeys in North Africa and America on her own. Simone was anxious that all her considerable experiences of life and voyages would vanish with her death. While discussing her intimacy with Sylvie Le Bon in *All Said and Done*, she says that never in her wildest dreams had she imagined that she would find a soulmate and colleague in her sixtieth year.

I drew two conclusions after reading her autobiographies—first, she wanted to remain independent, and second, one should seek to understand oneself truly. Simone was in a live-in relationship with Sartre but they never married because independence had different connotations for them. Simone writes that it was a unique independence. She was free of her past and felt complete and determined. She created her own space with immediacy; nobody could deprive her of it. On the other hand, Sartre, because he was a man, would hardly have achieved such a state, although he might have dreamt of it long ago. It was his foray into the world of adults, one which he abhorred with all his heart.

***

It is a pleasant April day. We travel the whole day by car. The sun is bright on the sea shore; a wide road runs along the coast to Rijeka. It is twenty-five degrees during the daytime and seven degrees at night. The glaring sun makes it tough to believe that hardly a couple of days ago the landscape was filled with the dazzle of snow and bone-chilling cold. Sasha and Kresho drive by turns. We make a couple of stops for gas. Sasha is bony. Chain smoking kills her hunger. She has wine in the car but I am famished. I bought a sandwich with cheese, hot chilli, and an olive slice filling at the petrol station. Sometimes, even the plebeian dry *roti* and *bhujia* become the most coveted delicacy.

We come across the castle of King Krešimir on the way. A market is held inside. Jewellery, paintings, statuettes of Mother Mary, idols of medieval soldiers with their full, club-like thighs, books, cassettes, songs and music, and tourists. It is a backwater port; boats leave for Paris from the dock. The crossing takes a couple of hours. We reach the spot in Rijeka where the book will be released at three in the afternoon. Snacks have been arranged for guests. People stand in line to fill their plates. Their focus is on the food. Filling the belly seems more important than interaction. I must acclaim Kresho and Sasha's marketing strategy. Such a sizeable crowd would not have been possible without the temptation of hors d'oeuvres. In the milling crowd, an elderly person with a ruddy face and flared nostrils is stuffing cookies in his pockets furtively. The pockets of the coat are bulging. I shift my gaze hurriedly as my heart overflows with pity.

Rieka or Rijeka is the third largest city in Croatia. This coastal city is distinguished for its shipbuilding. It has a remarkable multilingual history. Ostrogoths, Lombards, Avars, Franks, and Croatians have inhabited this place since the fifth century. Naturally, several languages are spoken in Rijeka. Right up to the Second World War, it was primarily an Italian city. Many of its citizens were killed and injured in guerrilla wars and raids. Around 800 people were sent to concentration camps. At present, it comprises 82 per cent Croats, 6 per cent Serbs, 2-2.5 per cent Bosnians, and 2 per cent Italians. The book release ceremony of *Chitra* is scheduled in the public library.

The library is huge and well-laid but many of the rooms on the upper floors are locked. They house ancient manuscripts. The librarian tells me that the grant from the government is so paltry that it is impossible to maintain all the rooms. The language used in the release ceremony is Croatian but evidently, Tagore is quite popular here. I have been told that when Tagore came to Zagreb in 1926, he visited Rijeka too. The philosopher Pawao Wuk Pablowich (1894-1976) translated his *Geetanjali* into Croatian. It was serialised in the Zagreb daily, *The Morning Leaf*, in January 1914. Later on, Pawao also translated *Chitra*, *Malini*, and *Raja*. *Chitra* was staged in the Croatian National Theatre on several occasions in 1915. The liberals of Rijeka saw

Tagore as an apostle of peace and spiritualism in the post-World War I years. During the ceremony, someone mentions Kreshimir Barnowic (1894-1975), the actor who played a role in the first performance of *Chitra.* Whatever the reasons behind Tagore's popularity, one fact is certain—the shortlisting of the German nationalist writer Peter Rosegger in Scotland for the Nobel Prize but Tagore receiving it during the First World War made him a household name. Tagore might be unaware but the hosts tell me that the German press had launched a vicious attack on him after the award. Today, the Croatians don't even recall Peter; their sympathies lie decidedly with Rabindranath Tagore.

There were terribly few Christian intellectuals that appreciated *Geetanjali* simply as a work of literature. Most of them were impressed by his mysticism. The Croatians beheld Tagore as a person offering spiritual leadership to the war-scarred minds during his Europe tour in 1926. Many of his works such as *Ghare Baire* were translated into Croatian during this period and he also delivered lectures for two days at the Croatian Music Conservatory Hall. The lectures were translated extemporaneously into Croatian but Tagore did not like it. I am mentioning it here because what I speak will also be translated live into Croatian. I have to pause repeatedly during my lecture on the works of Gurudev and his bonds with Croatia. The faces in the audience are impassive and vacant. They respond only to the translation by the interpreter, now blinking, now their eyes widening, now narrowing. The rapport between the speaker and the listeners is dependent on apt communication. I am unable to fathom how far and how deeply they grasp my lecture. Sasha is the Master of the Ceremony and I am told that the audience wants to hear a poem by Tagore. I cannot say why but I prefer rendering his *Dhwanila Ahvan* (The call resonates) to his other verses:

Dhwanila ahvan madhur gambhir prabhat ambar majhe
Dike digantare bhuvan mandire shanti sangeet baje
Hero go antare aroop sundare—Nikhil sansaar param bandhure
Esho anandita Milan-angane shobhan mangal saaje
Kalush kalmash virodh vidwesh houk nihshesh

Chitte hok jata bighnu upgata nitya kalyan kaje
Swar tarangiya gao bihangam, purba pashchim bandhu sangam
Maitribandhanpunyamantra-pabitra visva samaje.

(The morning sky resonates with a call sweet and sombre
The anthem of peace fills all lands far and near
Behold the beauty inside your mind—your soul mate
Come to the fete of joy, dressed in your best
Let your mind be cleansed and hate disappear
Let your mind be fearless in good endeavours
Perching on the horizon where West meets East, sing out O bird,
Let the sacred chant of friendship spread all over the world.)

***

It is May. I feel a bit settled now as if accepting my destiny. Now I do not long for my dear ones with the same ardour. Is recollection merely a force of habit? When you see them or hear them, your yearning intensifies. The more you yearn, the stronger it gets. Yet, recollections hang on despite the disillusionment. A fellow constantly adrift in memories is considered a sentimental fool. How do intimate relationships change into a medium of barter when confronted by the harsh realities of life? You mope but the world moves on. The current in a stream does not tarry, it does not remain stationary for anyone to take a dip in the same mass of water and rejuvenate. Stagnant water rots and stinks. If one tries too hard, one gathers only tangled weed covered in slime and filth; the clean water would have already flowed down to the sea. If you long for too great an intimacy, you receive only disappointment.

When you are alone, you can relax—assured that there are no annoyances—and then you can plunge headlong into creativity and contemplation. Rilke once said, 'Ask yourself in the dead of the night, is it obligatory to write?' An artist escapes the world in order to perceive it in one's art. We cannot reconstruct the truth if we stand too close to it; to exit the self is the first requisite to resurrecting truth. It is necessary to exist but also to remain detached. Only then can we create genuinely. Only then can we discover the truth. However, I find it hard to achieve this artistic state. On the contrary, I have become an aggregate of the Croatian reality in my pursuit to distinguish it. I feel I have lived in this land for centuries among its women—the past is but a distant dream, as if it never was.

Anyway, I am trying to find out what Adriana Mestrovic had hinted at, without anticipating that in the coming months my inquisitiveness would get the better of me. I did not have much of an idea about Liliana's personal life; moreover, asking personal questions is not suitable etiquette. The great Hindi author, Premchand, too, believes that one must not ask embarrassing questions. I have begun to examine the changed conditions and circumstances in post-war Europe while re-reading Simone de Beauvoir and in the process, I have stumbled upon a door, albeit a closed one—Liliana's life. Mariana has told me she is a war victim. Lily or Dushka can tell me what I need to know. Dushka is way too sentimental. She may get offended. Scouring one's own wounds privately is one thing and presenting them for public demonstration is another. Liliana likes to meet foreigners, especially the dusky ones. I have some pearl ornaments from Hyderabad. I have gift-wrapped them and decided to visit her with Dushka. Lily is a robust woman, in the pink of health, around fifty. She buys only white toilet paper because she believes coloured paper can cause cancer. Her hair is golden white, like flax. She is wearing a deep magenta lipstick, and her neck and the upper part of her bosom are bare in the bitterest of colds. When she comes across people, she holds up her head and loose bust proudly. She frequents the elite circle in her high heels and short skirt. Her mannerisms are not something I am acquainted with. Women were victimised by the Serb military in Croatia and Bosnia-Herzegovina in 1992-95—Lily is one of them. During the war, thousands of cases of sexual violence were reported, some of them were buried in red tape, some were forgotten, and some were withdrawn. A few women were killed. Some fell victim to depression and other illnesses. Although sexual violence and individual or gang rape by soldiers during a war is considered a heinous war crime in the Geneva Convention, the sexual persecution of women during a war is an unwritten part of their history.

Rape in war is considered something different from rape during normal times. Several of these cases are not even investigated. Many a time the victims do not even complain. Liliana is one of the exceptional ones that did not bow to the times or the circumstances. Instead of choosing cautiously between life, death, and silence, she reported the crimes of mass rapes that had taken place extensively. During the First and Second World Wars, the military and the para-military forces in several countries perpetrated this crime regularly. In the First World War, Belgium and Russia turned into mass killing fields for women. During the Second World War, women were raped on an unprecedented scale in Russia, Japan, Italy, Korea, China, the Philippines, and Germany. There is a long list of such atrocities in the countless major and minor skirmishes in Afghanistan, Algeria, Argentina, Bangladesh, Brazil, Bosnia, Cambodia, Congo, Croatia, Cyprus, El Salvador, Guatemala, Haiti, India, Indonesia, Kuwait, Colombo, Liberia, Mozambique, Nicaragua, Peru, Pakistan, Rwanda, Serbia, Somalia, Turkey, Uganda, Vietnam, and Zimbabwe but the voices of protest were suppressed under lengthy sermons and political compromises. Wislawa Szymborska's poem, *Vietnam*, is about the women victims of war crimes,

Woman, by what name should I call you?
I don't know
How old are you? From which land do you come?
I don't know
Why did you dig this trench?
I don't know
How long will you remain in hiding?
I don't know.
Why did you bite my finger?
I don't know
Don't you know that we were not the one to hurt you?
I don't know
Which side do you belong to?
I don't know
But this is war, you must choose
I don't know
Do you miss your village?
I don't know
Are these your kids?
Yes.
(Translated from Aparna Manoj's Hindi version)

***

I no longer find Liliana's shaking of her legs while listening to the concert, her chain-smoking, her grin, and her wink weird. The owner of the four-star hotel in Spilt is head over heels in love with Lily. Liliana says she would go to Spilt in the summers and earn enough for the whole year. She is an escort. Businessmen and tourists spend a lot on escort services. Liliana never talks about herself seriously. She has suffered sexual violence and gang rapes. She laughs at life. Many of her companions in Zagreb, too, were raped by the Serb soldiers. Some of them were held captive in the army camps as sex slaves. There are a large number of old women who witnessed these atrocities. Many of the abused young women became pregnant; a few of them chose abortion over shame and ignominy. Some gave birth to children but sent them hastily to government orphanages. Lily's only son, an inmate at the government drug rehabilitation centre, was born in 1996. Liliana remembers each small detail, but she avoids recounting them. I do not pester her and return to my flat.

***

I cannot sleep. What was the fate of hundreds of women like Liliana? What terrible trauma did they undergo? I am stifled in the inkiest darkness; there are no faces, only groans. Viktor Frankl wrote *Man's Search for Meaning* after the Second World War; it is his journal of the concentration camp at Auschwitz. Frankl notes that the life span of a prisoner was dependent on the way he visualised his future. He speaks about Logotherapy and asserts that those who want to live, do live under any circumstance. What motivation did these sex slaves have? They were stripped right before their husbands, children, mothers, and mothers-in-law and raped, month after month, year after year; there was no end to their abuse and ordeals. What hope did they nurture after all? I see the Auschwitz concentration camp in my half-sleep. Restless, perspiring, and panicky...Liliana is trying to escape with her child in her lap. By the barbed fence, there is an endless mob—fair, ruddy faced, looming soldiers. They are stripping Liliana, dragging her, spitting in her face, spreading her legs. She is shrieking like a cow in labour. They rape her one by one. Lily...Lily... Liliana...I am startled awake by my own cry...I get up and look at the screen of my phone...there are a couple of messages...I take a swig of water. I remember a couplet,

> *Tumi guchiye kichhu katha bolte paro na*
> *Shudhu samay nijer galpa bole jay*
> (You can never organise your words/but time flows on, telling its own stories.)

Right it is, am I really writing systematically? Women like Liliana have snatched away my peace. I keep thinking about them all the time. I want to know more. It appears only time will write their story anyway, when will this moment come?

***

I have spent the last week in weird loneliness. Examinations are on so there are no classes. I had only two chores—translating and chronicling the diary. There is no alternative to human presence. If two persons understand each other, they become an entire universe. Guldane Kalin, from Izmir in Turkey, teaches Turkish and English; she is a decent and considerate woman. We often meet at the university. Gul understands me. Liliana and Igor have invited me to a party this Saturday. I am on the horns of a dilemma. My vegetarian, teetotaller Indian upbringing smirks. If Baba or my siblings find out, they will be incredulous. Liliana tells me I might come across women willing to talk about their experiences.

We go to Shalata, from where we have to move on to the pot party. I don't know much about it, but the moment I stepped in I felt suffocated by the toxic smoke. There was a huge crowd, most of them girls, smoking pot. I felt my head spinning without inhaling a single puff. People lie silently—some are gazing at the ceiling, some are smoking. There is light music. When I preened my ears, I made out it was the chime of '*Hare Rama...Hare Krishna*', the tune that plays in the religious assemblies of Sri Sri Ravi Shankar. A strong urge to run away grips me. It was a terrible mistake to come to this suffocating party...oh, I shouldn't have! A pair is leaning against the wall. The boy walks up to me and says something, touching my hair gently, '*Gelim dotaknutiswoze kren dlake*' (I want to touch your brunette hair). I dart outside as if escaping the pits of hell. Liliana and Igor are nowhere to be seen. I change three trams and sink into deep sleep at home, reassured by a sense of security. The following Sunday Liliana laughs, '*Nemozte seprepala*', do not be afraid. 'Nobody will force you, your hair is black, and it is a curiosity here'.

***

The tram turns on its tracks set in the middle of the iron bricks of the street as it travels to Turkebana Yelachica. There are large, tall glass doors in the circular building, and it is filled with shops. Woollen, cotton dresses carrying tags of 'Made in China' or 'Made in India'. The footwears are from Vietnam and Thailand. The face of the shopkeeper resembles that of a fox without a tail. Deep set green eyes and a red nose on a flat face, he appears polite but there seems to be something simmering in his head crowned with reddish-brownish hair—I believe it is racism. He does not consider a coloured person worthy of respect. I can sense it. A white young boy with a freckled face, hardly six or seven, is pushing his nose against the window pane outside. He is wearing a cloak-like garment, outsized, split shoes are on his feet. He lopes away like a rabbit when he espies the shopkeeper moving towards him. Next to it is the renowned cake shop of Zagreb. Croatian and German cakes fill the see-through shelves in full glory, waiting for customers with stuffed pockets. Guldane Kalin has often recommended the pastry from this shop. I should enjoy it today. The speciality of these cakes is their cream topping, tempting one's palate and weight control. A beautiful, well-garnished, cream covered, encrusted large piece lies on my plate. It cost 50 kunas, around 500 rupees. It would cost the same at a Barista in my own country.

I slice the first piece when the manager-sort guy in the shop shoos away the child standing outside. The little kid has walked into the shop with a torn packet of potato chips. An employee drags him by his cloak, the siren begins to hoot. The kid is dumb, and by the time I reach him, he has been kicked out on the road like a football. When I ask, he points at the garbage bin. He is weeping and crying loudly, '*jasam gladna*' (I am hungry). I guess he might have picked up the half-eaten chips packet discarded by someone to satisfy his hunger and the shopkeeper would have caught him. My appetite for the cake is gone. Perhaps I will never taste it now. The kid's nose is soaked in blood. I buy some cake for him. He is sobbing. He is probably a refugee. The white topping on the cake clenched in his fist is turning red slowly. Oh, God! How many of these kids have become castaways? Without a life of dignity, without food, without a roof! There are NGOs and governments, but lost in our cushy world, do we ever cast a single glance at them? My heart sobs. The rain has started pattering outside.

Be by my side, I am scared
Maybe this moment is not real
Hold me tight
Like holding a dead body at the crematorium
Folks and kin,
Take my hand
Keep holding it while you are here
Don't let go
I am afraid
Maybe this moment is not real
Like the last, false, lingering one or like the false, infinite future.
(Nabaneeta Dev Sen)

I talk to my sister over the phone. She advises me to return to India before I become a victim of abysmal depression. She is quite worried about me. Her experience of raising a family has jump-started her maturity. Whenever I talk about the experiences of war and the problems of women, her artist heart quivers. She has written that I must return quickly.

I wrote back today—

> Dear Ukki,
>
> I am better now. I am trying to find out more about the women war victims. Don't worry about me because there are Dushka, Liliana, Guldane, and Kresho to take care of me here. Despite the fact that I have lost five kgs, I am fine. Most of the things I had brought from India are still lying unused. I have turned off the heating knob in one of the rooms to preserve the eatables. There are plenty of shops around filled with snacks but whenever I think of buying them, I remember you, as if we are still children, sharing our toffees. Had you been here, we would have enjoyed ourselves a whole heap, stuffing ourselves, making long trips. Fighting, going on buying sprees. I am really a gullible customer because so far you have bought everything for me. The moment I see some beautiful object on a shop shelf, I imagine you are standing beside me. I believe it is only you who are waiting for me; everyone else must be lost in their own life. I talked to Papa in Delhi on Skype. I must say, Papa will never understand his daughters. He believes I should not have taken up this assignment. Moreover, in

our country, daughters are not preferred; their birth is always considered an accident. But the world I see these days, the kind of people I meet, our past, our small discomforts and slights are nothing compared to theirs. How could I have realised it if I had not come here?

Last week I visited the rehabilitation centre in Zagreb, the place where women learn small crafts like packaging, making pickles, jams, spices, etc. to earn a livelihood. Serbia had set up 480 civil and military prison camps during the Bosnia-Herzegovina and Croatia war. The Croatian and Bosnian citizens were intimidated through the rape of their women. Small groups of attackers targeted villages, and girls and women were their first prey. Gang rapes were undertaken publicly to warn other villages. Serb soldiers publicly demonstrated sexual abuse of women on a large scale in military camps, hotels, and brothels between 1991 and 1995. As long as Serbia controlled Bosnia and Herzegovina, no woman, irrespective of her age, was spared. Liliana and Dushka found jobs in the tourism department and came to Zagreb. They were Croatian citizens despite being Serbs; moreover, they were girls—fresh, live, succulent flesh. Liliana was one of those unfortunate women who were tormented, beaten, and imprisoned. Many girls were forced into obscene sexual demonstrations, their private parts were branded with burning cigarettes, and they were raped multiple times every day. This rehabilitation centre had helped such women to become self-dependent; it is still operational.

As soon as the war touched a village, families would run away. What remained behind were the farmlands, livestock, and captured women, aged ten to seventy. This brutalisation was termed a war crime internationally but no definite government policy evolved even after the war for these abused women. Many countries, for example, the Soviet Union, used rape as a weapon to subjugate Germany in the Second World War. Similarly, Bangladeshi women were raped by Pakistani soldiers on a massive scale. We are also familiar with the sexual abuse of women in the Ugandan civil war and Iran. Mass rape of women by the Japanese militia in China's Nanking, their conquests, and sexual abuse of Sri Lankan women during neo-imperialism were also used as ruinous weapons. Several feminists tried to gather consensus against such incidents through documentaries and films, however, Bosnian and Herzegovinian women never became an issue for serious international deliberations.

Therefore, I plan to visit Bosnia first, and Croatia next. I may be off the grid for a few days, don't get anxious if I don't communicate. Take care. Send emails. I will look them up in some internet café.

Love.

***

Getting permission from the embassy to visit Bosnia was

easy but the senior officials mocked me, 'People go to Paris, Italy, and Germany, but you are dying to meet the war victims'. Bosnia is supposedly suffering from plunder, corruption, and petty crimes but the road passing through the green farmlands seems to belie it. Liliana and Bozac are with me. On the wrong side of fifty, Bozac, a Bosnian student, studies and works in Zagreb. His wife and his eight-year-old daughter were ravaged repeatedly before his eyes. The little girl was soaked in blood, but the soldiers kept tossing her around for three days. Nobody knew when she breathed her last. Bozac points out the spot where his wife had died from depression and a heart condition. He laughs bitterly with a cryptic 'life must go on', and leads me on to the next concentration camp. After they lost their daughter, his wife kept praying to Lord Jesus to confess her uncommitted crimes. What was her crime? Bozac responds, 'Being a woman'.

The women that were abused physically over and over again—fouled by the loathsome semen of malicious soldiers—bore the war on their bodies even after the ceasefire, suffering various cardiac and mental ailments. In Rwanda, 5,000 children were born out of rape during the 1994 civil war. No NGO was able to assess their numbers in Croatia because most of the cases were hushed up. The neighbours and the relatives also ducked the question. The war had invaded everyone's mind and heart. Most of the raped women suffered from death guilt. They refused to open up. Many just stared into the void for years. Some lost their voice. A few left their houses and never had sex again. According to a rough estimate, around

50,000 girls and women were raped during the war in Bosnia. Ironically, the International Criminal Tribunal for the Former Yugoslavia simply kept printing ream after ream on the issue of sex slavery, terming rape 'a crime against humanity'.

United Yugoslavia was split into five sovereign countries—Bosnia and Herzegovina, Croatia, Macedonia Republic, Slovenia, and the Federal Republic of Yugoslavia. Later on, the Federal Republic was further divided into Serbia, Montenegro, and Kosovo. Most of the battles and clashes occurred for territory. Even today, there are more than 7,000 Croatian refugees in Bosnia and Herzegovina. Around 131,600 people were displaced. Croatia and Bosnia share 935 kilometres of border.

We have been warned repeatedly against cons by the Croatian Embassy in Sarajevo. On the road, our passports and visas are checked several times. The rundown communication means and roads remind me of the small towns back in India. There are landmines around. The police stop and interrogate us for hours. The older generation does not understand or speak English, only the young ones do. Many Bosnians had sought asylum in Germany during the war, this is why they use German words abundantly. We get an invitation to go rafting on the Una River, but I decline.

***

Yesterday Lily (Liliana) emailed me the piece 'Life of Miranda', published in the *Los Angeles Times* in 1993. When I returned to my hotel, I went through it:

Every night the White Eagles picked us up and dropped us back the next morning. Sometimes there were more than twenty. The things they did to us cannot be described in words. I don't even want to remember it. We had to cook and serve food without a stitch on our bodies. They raped and killed numerous girls right before our eyes; those that resisted, their breasts were chopped off.

These women, numbering around 1,000, were captured from different towns and villages. I spent four months in the camp. One night, the brother of our Serbian neighbour helped twelve of us to escape. Two of them were recaptured. We remained hidden in the forest for days. If the neighbour had not helped us, I too would have died. Most probably I would have killed myself. The tortures I suffered were worse than death.

Sometimes I am afraid the nightmares won't ever spare me. Every night I am haunted by the face of the camp sentry, Stozan. He was the most merciless. He did not spare even a ten-year-old girl. Most of the little girls died writhing after rape. They killed many. I want to forget all this anyhow, or else I will die!

***

My heart is choking. I have lost my appetite. I seek the shelter of Skype. No friend, no relative is online. It is said there is no fate worse than being without a friend. I peer outside the window. The streetlights have come on. The lights switch on automatically as soon as darkness falls, even if it is only the clouds. There is a hush all around. The bright red light on top of the Viesnik D.D. building looks like a lighthouse beacon in the middle of a boundless ocean. It must be midnight back in India. '*Megher pare megh jamechhe andhakare ase*' (Clouds pile up on clouds, darkness descends). I wake up instinctively whenever clouds cover the sky, their clammy smell makes me restless even in sleep. I munch on two biscuits and gulp down swigs of water, but I am still fidgety. I imagine gigantic, burly, ruthless Serbian soldiers riding the soughing, viscous winds blowing in from across the Balkans. Pitiful cries rent the air.

A schoolgirl from Foka in 1992 discloses how a fellow called Zoran Wukovich forced himself upon her and then threw her before others. A posse of soldiers marched into the school premises and ordered eight girls to remove their undergarments and lie down on the floor. The girls were raped repetitively before the entire class. The soldiers picked out Bosniak girls and shoved their penis in their mouths, 'You Muslim whores, we will show you what it is!' She has no words to describe the atrocity, she just keeps repeating, 'Nothing can be worse for a woman'.

Later, she was held hostage in Patrizen Sports Hall with around sixty other women of varying ages. They would be picked up by turn by the soldiers and imprisoned in the sports hall once they had been ravaged and bloodied. The Serb militia had converted houses, offices, and many of the schools into concentration camps. One of the Bosnian women reported that on the first day, all the menfolk of the house were rounded up and thrashed savagely. 'My mother ran away—we never could find her again despite our best efforts. They ravaged me. I fell unconscious from pain and fear...when I came to, I found myself lying naked in a pool of my own blood on the floor...my sister-in-law suffered a similar fate...I realised I had been raped...in one corner of the house my mother-in-law was crying with the baby in her lap...we were held captive in our own houses. It was the vilest hour of my life...they would parade and offer us to the soldiers. Back in the house too, they forced us to indulge in outrageous acts, violating us...in front of our children. It continued for a whole year, most of the women succumbed or went mad or turned prostitutes.'

The Dayton Accords peace treaty, inked after the war, carried the provision of compensating the abused women with houses and other properties but hardly any of them was willing to return. Most of them refused to come back to their houses because the structures were now painful reminders of their torment and a forfeited past.

***

Hasesis, a gorgeous-looking cherubic woman with lustrous, pink skin, runs a bistro. She has won several prizes in culinary arts. We are at her restaurant for lunch. She smiles bashfully when she finds a foreigner in the group and receives us warmly. She knows a little English. Her head is covered with a green scarf, and her petite hands and feet seem to be carved from butter. At my insistence, she finally agrees to talk about herself at three in the afternoon, the lean hours. Three women work in the well-kept restaurant—Hasesis handles the cash register, greeting all the guests with a smile. There are chairs inside and outside the bistro and pots of seasonal flowers adorn every corner. The mixed fragrance of the charcoal from the sizzlers and the fresh fried ice cream in a large pan is irresistible. Liliana is fond of vanilla ice cream fried in a batter of eggs and dry fruits. It is said that Nero used to serve ice cream fritters to his soldiers in Rome. The recipe has gone through lots of experimentation. Hasesis serves it with thick chocolate sauce.

It is only half past one in the afternoon; I can sit and while away the hours until Hasesis is free. The chairs are plastic, but they look like cane. There is an umbrella over every table to protect the customers from the sun. We can hear the strums of a guitar from across the street; an avant-garde sort of fellow is strumming and singing. He has unfolded his jacket on the ground and a couple of coins are lying on it. We stroll in the direction. When he opens an English number, Liliana smiles. I follow him easily, it is *Hotel California*,

> On a dark desert highway, cool wind in my hair
> Warm smell of colitas, rising up through the air
> Up ahead in the distance, I saw a shimmering light
> My head grew heavy and my sight grew dim
> I had to stop for the night.
> There she stood in the doorway;
> I heard the mission bell
> And I was thinking to myself

'This could be Heaven or this could be Hell'
Then she lit up a candle and she showed me the way
There were voices down the corridor,
Though I heard them say
Welcome to the Hotel California
Such a lovely place, such a lovely place
Such a lovely face.
Plenty of room at Hotel California
Any time of the year, any time of the year, you can find
it here.

Whenever I hear this track by the Eagles, I feel I am hearing it afresh. It won a Grammy in 1978. The song sounds magical on the guitar. Liliana too is lost in the lyrics. Melody can lift us to a superior plane of consciousness. The songwriter of *Hotel California*, Don Henley, has said that it is the song of a chaste journey—priceless, like an experience.

The audience has started clapping and the singer's face glows with pleasure, his eyes sparkle with a canny business sense. I drop a twenty kuna note. He begins a Hrvatski number. Humming the tune, we return to Hasesis who has removed her apron and brushed her hair. We decide to sit inside the restaurant.

Hasesis has been unable to erase the memory of April 1992, even after so many years. With obvious reluctance, she lets us record her words. Liliana interprets. Hasesis remembers the day distinctly when Serb soldiers dragged her to the basement of the Vizegrad police station. 'It was crammed with wooden furniture, chairs, etc. I saw Milan Lusik and Strezo Lusik there. I knew Milan very well but he waved a knife in my face, growling, "Take off your clothes". At first, I thought it was a joke. The reality was that my old Serbian neighbour was bent on devastating me in collusion with the soldiers.' Hasesis does not actually remember how many days she remained a prisoner in the basement. In the following days, the moment she heard the voices of the Serbian neighbours, she would remove her clothes and lie down on the floor. The sooner the torture got over, the better it was.

She was given food only once in the whole day. The Serb soldiers were so vicious that she had decided that she would offer no resistance at all. The moment one was done with her, she would beckon another. In this manner, she saved herself from the whippings. She says that she was convinced the torture would end eventually and she would be able to go back to her little babies. Liliana asks her how painful it was. Hasesis replies, 'When I lay under them, I felt I was a gutter overflowing with sewage; it had to get over one day. It was the innocent face of my little girl that fortified my resolution. Still, when I returned home, my husband divorced me because I had gone frigid in bed. However, now I work hard, and I have given a good life to my children'.

How simple it is to hear these words, how grim to go through the travails! Of all the human values, courage is the finest, without it, you never can protect any other virtue. You may be sincere, benevolent, confident, or loving, but to be any of these you have to stand fearless first. Bravery is not merely stepping into the battlefield; it means the fortitude within, something that makes your strength visible to others. You need guts to have this kind of courage. Insignificant people like us magnify our small discomforts and misery out of proportion. But this woman who suffered the foulest of tortures, she is building her life anew to carry on with gusto.

***

Yesterday we went to the spa resort Vilina Vlas, a huge tourist attraction. It is a swanky joint. Liliana knows the staff members through her profession. Maybe she often comes to this place. Besides, the hotel people supply clients to her. Thankfully, my colleagues at Zagreb University do not have any inkling of the kind of places I am visiting or else it would not take them long to preach to me. Surprisingly, both genders are equally adept at moral policing. Keep yourself locked in the house, don't meet strangers, don't go to unfamiliar places, and in the event that you have to, please ask someone to accompany you—such sermons are common. If you listen to them, you won't get anywhere because you may not find a worthy chaperon every time. Moreover, what you seek may not concern your escort.

It is hard to believe that 200 women were kept captive once in this hotel. I come across the elderly janitor—a woman—who works here to keep her body and soul together. She remembers the incidents clearly although she is not sure about the date, 'I escaped into the forest with my sixteen-year-old son but hid my daughter in the house because I had heard that they were kidnapping girls. They threatened and unclothed me before my son and slashed his throat with a knife. "Mumma"—this was his last word. Sometimes they took me to the camp for a couple of days and then dropped me back at the hotel. I lost count of how many times I was raped. All the hotel rooms were locked from the outside; they threw down bread from the window. We held the bread with our teeth because our hands were tied behind our backs. We were untied only when they wanted to rape us. We lost track of time. Sometimes we were burnt with cigarettes; sometimes they bit flesh from our tongues. Most of us women did not speak or weep. Several committed suicide, while some perished from hunger and pain. Many women were raped continuously for seven to nine hours. Some of the acts were filmed for the pornography market'. I do not know how to jot it down. Alexander Pope has said that it is quite difficult to read easy writing, but the reverse is also true—that which reads easy is hard to write. This old woman who works here to make ends meet, what hope has she left in her life? I cannot talk directly to her because of the language barrier, but in her eyes, I can discern a weird desolation. People can forget oral accounts, but an experience can never be blotted out. I hand her a hundred kunas. A smile appears on the lips of the old woman, she tucks it hastily inside her blue uniform and dashes down the stairs with her cleaning bucket. Windfall income does inspire a rush of energy.

***

Since these rapes were committed by individuals and not by a government agency, several international organisations held the view that it was not an infringement of human rights. Later on, when the Bosnian government termed the violence of the Serb soldiers as genocide in the International Court of Justice, and when the United Nations announced the formation of the International War Crime Tribunal in 1993, for the first time, some of the cases were taken up. Sometimes the victim refused to identify the perpetrator. Often the charges were withdrawn. It is a curious fact that the Tribunal lacked funds for the hearings—a fact confirmed by a report published in the *New York Times* on December 7, 1994. It was outrageous that there were only three women on the eighteen-member committee of the tribunal.

After protracted sessions, twenty-one Serb commandos were finally held guilty of operating concentration camps and perpetrating violence in Bosnia. The court observed that women were not only held hostages in Omarska Camp but also raped and killed. Many of them were battered and they also suffered other barbaric acts. The international human rights acts expert in New York, Ronda Komplon, believed that it was unethical to reveal the identity of the victims without their consent. There were very few women in the Muslim-majority population of Bosnia that stepped forward to identify their rapists.

Bozac takes me to Semka. I record her statements. Semka Ezik, around fifty-five, has spent her life in a small town, Jivinay, in north-east Bosnia. She shudders, 'Whenever I narrate my experiences, I begin to sweat and my head spins. I have to take medicine beforehand to check the spells'.

***

Semka describes her experiences in graphic detail—it has made me restive. There is a bitter taste in my mouth; panic grips me when I recline on my left side. During this trip, I have not been able to sleep peacefully even once—my appetite is gone too. I eat only rice and curd as the staple food here is non-vegetarian. I do not feel like eating as I write the diary and the descriptions at night. A group of Serb para-military forces dispatched Semka Ezik to Zasa Wic in July 1992. Her teenage son Dwejad was shot dead. Overwhelmed by grief and insensate, Semka blurts out, 'I had no idea a worse fate awaited me'. She was confined in an empty house with a group of women in Zasa Wic. Drunk Serb soldiers hustled them one by one into a room at gunpoint—'Shall I shoot you?' The story of her physical abuse continued until she was released in a mutual exchange of Bosnian and Serb prisoners. Semka does not expect justice to come her way. Earning a living from animal husbandry and farming, she is poised on an endless wait for a son who will never return. Her village neighbours say, 'For several months, she would stay put at the bus stand the whole day, expecting her son to arrive on one of the buses. Her medical treatment finally made her realise the truth; however, she is not normal, even now'.

***

I had always thought that the women in Europe lead a better life than their Asian counterparts but this alluring beer-producing country clearly has a dormant history inscribed in blood. In India, millions of people lost their homes when Bengal was divided; around 100,000 women suffered physical exploitation and sexual violence. Why do such things happen? It does not matter where a war is taking place or who the warring factions are, it is the women who suffer ultimately. I once saw a movie, *The Children of War*. It is a record of the atrocities committed by the military, in quest of a greater nation. During the 1971 Indo-Pak war, the Pak military victimised mostly non-Sunni Muslims and Bengali Hindus. The rape of women was a demonstration of their jihadi attitude which believes that forced sexual relations can expunge a whole race.

A woman is considered nothing more than a womb, she is only a vessel for receiving sperm—willingly or unwillingly. She is the one who is vanquished. The offenders believe that the children born out of rape shall carry forward their DNAs and shall display a similarly sectarian mindset. Diverse religions throughout the globe have proliferated on the basis of such a creed. The most monstrous manifestation of this in India was effected by the Portuguese in Goa, where they were given free rein to rape Indian women in order to breed Portuguese offspring. It was a variety of religious genocide.

***

The last month was not a happy one. The more I learn

about Bosnia-Herzegovina, the more restless and inquisitive I become. This is probably why Adorno announced after Auschwitz that poetry had died. My mind is a whirlwind. Ukki whispers to me, 'Simone's translation has made you miserable, or else your cheerfulness was contagious. It has happened after your return from Bosnia. You need to forget the past and take a break because these experiences now haunt your dreams all the time'.

***

I am reading Croatian poets. Ivan Goran Kovacic, a twentieth century poet, has unsettled me. His poem recounts the extremes of the tortures during the Second World War.

> Blood seeps in the light of the day, in the gloam of the night
> It is the destiny of a night stapled on my cheeks.
> I see through the mind's eyes
> Tears don't roll out from my eye sockets, though flames shoot out
> My heart is fidgety, my breath stutters,
> And my shining, liquid, curious eyes die by the moment
> In the cup of my palm.

Sentiments of banishment, anguish, and exploitation overflow in the Croatian poems—Ivan Goran Kovacic is an integral part of the curriculum in Croatia. Another poet, Drubawka Euresik, whose poetry is mostly about exile, has received a number of international awards. Ivan Slamnig (1930-2001) was a veteran poet and translator. He took up the vital chore of translating books of English literature into Croatian to introduce the new generation to world writings. I am reading his *Entolozia Hrvatska Poezie*, an anthology of the first generation Croatian poets in the first half of the nineteenth century. I also like *Wounded Cannon* by Ranjini Tenk.

I want to read Slavenka Drakulich because Sergei Mikhailic has told me that her novels and essays expound the orientation of feminist discourses and the political spectrum in the whole of Europe. These days, haiku is quite the rage in Croatia, and haiku contests are held regularly. Vladimir Devide, a mathematician, pioneered haiku poetry in this country. Jwonko Petrovic and Tomislav Maretic have taken it to new heights. Tomislav is a doctor by profession and a poet by heart, and he questions me eagerly about India. I understand that he wants his haiku to reach Indian readers too—translation is an interesting activity if you want to brighten your mood. It does not matter how tense you are, the moment you take the helm, you begin to live—your concentration and your consciousness flow and synchronise into your hands, feet, and eyes. Maretic writes,

> In spite of all that happened
> His dog
> Still wags his tail when he sees me
> Still.

And this second haiku,

> Dark

Seabird
Dips in the ocean
The ocean turns dark.

The bird that I have called 'Dark Seabird' in the second haiku is actually the finch, with a tiny beak and golden black feathers. I remember Sergei after a long while as I read his poems and sit down to write an email to him.

For the last few months, I have not been much in touch with my Indian friends, in fact, the family folk come up with the same clichéd questions and replies. Does physical distance really rob the warmth of a relationship?

Dear Sergei Mikhailic,

I am fine, Ivan was a great help. Your appraisal of Croatian poets is correct. Recently, I read several haikus and now I am translating them.

I never stop thinking that I am in an alien land. Sometimes, a poem moistens my eyes and my vision blurs, reviving the past on the screen of my eyes once again. You were right in your remark, 'This is not how a seasoned tourist behaves'. Let us talk about poetry, there is a lot of variety in Tomislav Maretitc's haikus, their brevity holds you sharply albeit his conversation tends to be more gripping. He comes up with lengthy speeches on literature, history, culture, and medicine—sometimes they turn monotonous with a surfeit of information. We meet often in the coffee house. It is hard to find seats, but once Doctor Tomislav grabs one, he can spend hours talking over a cup. Ivan Andreic knows why I speak to him about the violence in wars for hours. Nowadays he ducks the subject. People in your country are experts in hiding the past. Had it been my country, the betel seller on the street or even the locality barber would have described the local history juicily.

There are three of us around the table in the coffee house but only one person speaks—Tomislav. I had always thought that women were great talkers, but now I realise that an apparently solemn man, too, can speak for hours on end. Luckily, I have an antidote. If I need to learn more about Serbia and Croatia, I have to listen to the doctor's bloats of creativity patiently. After his bountiful Sunday homilies, he is assured that Ivan and I are good listeners and that we dare not run away from his tedium. Maybe I have inherited my father's patience a tad. Maretic enjoys black coffee, Ivan prefers beer, and I nibble on the povitica almond and honey soaked bread. A hot coffee is most welcome. Maretic sips his coffee, now gone cold from his hours of talk on the world. This culture of meeting people in the coffee house is not really bad. At least here you aren't bothered about your curtains, your doors and windows, and the sofa sets for the guests; neither do you have to worry about the dishes or your dresses. Coffee houses are open round the clock every kilometre or a half—just don a dress, snatch an umbrella, see people, and then come back to your nest. Coffee houses have been a great support to women's liberation.

You can tick off your closest pal without any offence—Tomislav sees his two former wives in the coffee house itself; the third one does not even have an inkling of the meetings, he personally told me this. He talks to his former wives in the coffee house; he asks about the children, advises them, and thus safeguards himself against all the uncomfortable queries that might confront him at home. In the course of his talks, sometimes he gets excited and imagines himself to be a warrior. He has great faith in his own writings. He says one thing and then comes up with a different theory and after he has carried an argument to finality, he backtracks. For example, 'I can do this…had I done this…', and then he would discuss its negatives to underpin his logic. Sometimes I understand him, sometimes I don't. Often, he quotes lines from poems—he has a wonderful memory!

How are you? The library is shut these days so the books I had borrowed from you are still with me. I will return them soon. How is your white cat Liasa? I really find it weird that you and your wife have not gone out together for thirty-five years, simply for the sake of your cat. Perhaps I would not have dared to say this to you personally, but I have taken the liberty of doing it in the email. Please don't mind.

With regards,

Your Garry.

***

This week I have planned to see Tomislav Maretic in the coffee house located on the street that runs along River Sawa, turning in from the tenth intersection on Ivana Ulichica. I bolster myself. Since he is quite learned, I am certain I will get replies to all my queries. At times he poses awkward questions about India, and I find it hard to answer them with any certainty. It vexes me because I do not like avoiding issues. We meet in the café on the appointed day. It is not crowded this afternoon. There are a few students from the Philosophy Facultat, the place where I work, but they seem indifferent. I too overlook them. Of course, they are not Indian students that naturally bubble with excitement when they come across their teachers, then smile and greet them, look shyly and curiously at their companion, hazard a guess, and then greet you with a *namaste* and a beaming grin.

We order coffee. The young man at the coffee counter is handsome; he pours and serves green coffee in cups. Tomislav is quieter today. Anxieties mount if a fellow has to maintain more than one wife and family. I believe that if one cannot handle a single marriage, he should not be too adventurous. It is better to be by oneself. However, as a fellow who is accustomed to living in a family, it must be hard for him to remain alone. It is more true for a man, that he needs a woman at every stage of life—mother, sister, mate, serf—it must be more testing for him to be alone than a woman. It is a personal conviction. I have switched on the recorder, but Tomislav's replies are fragmentary. He is convinced that the exploitation and suffering of war can never be compensated. He very reluctantly agrees to take me to his neighbour Emina Rahmanovic, who was separated from her family on the Bosnia-Croatia frontier in 1992 when she was hardly fifteen. Her family was one of the thousands of refugees that had bribed their way into Croatia, but Emina's dire destiny cast her into the army barracks of Travonic, where the winter of 1993 devastated her life. When she left for Zenika, she was alone, ill, and pregnant—gifts of abuse she had received from the war. The twins, son and daughter, were raised in an orphanage.

Tomislav stops speaking. I suggest to Ivan we should get hold of Emina. I get the phone number of Emina's husband from Tomislav. Ivan will escort me there next Wednesday. Although Emina's house is in the lower town, Rolda has told me she would come with us so we must go to the upper town first to pick her up. Rolda had taught the Dutch language in India for a few months. She has a treasure trove of vicarious experiences. I decide to reach Rolda by tram; Ivan will drive to her house. The plan is finalised. Rolda has promised to show me a museum of ruined loves. It was opened recently, in 2010, set up by a couple that broke up despite their vows of undying love until eternity. They explored the whole world to collect a phenomenal number of legends, amour gifts, and pictures of wrecked love. We lark a good deal over the tokens of shattered hearts. When I ask Rolda about her personal life, she grins, 'My granny's flat is here in Zagreb. She had laid down the condition that the relative who would take care of her in her old days would inherit the flat. I agreed and now I need not worry about a house'. What about love? It trickled in in bits and pieces. If one of her paramours was already hitched, another was a divorcee. The pursuit of the PhD degree ushered into her an intellectual tranquillity, replacing tantrums and over-sensitivity. When she went to India on a teaching assignment, she was mesmerised by the black eyes of the Indians. She had several liaisons in India. Twice she almost committed herself to live-in relationships, however, the gentleman was partial to girls from exotic lands, and he would lie in her guest room bed with the shoes on. He spent all his time at her place—breakfast to dinner. He was always asking her to fetch things, pestering her. 'Rolda, where are my clothes? Rolda, will brown shoes go with this shirt?' He would bring along his friends in the evenings to show off that he was living with a white girl. She tolerated him for a month and then kicked him out. The poor fellow was bawling as he packed his suitcase.

'After that, I shunned closeness with Indian men. Do you know Garry? Most Indian men seek a mother in their wives and girlfriends, one who will look after him like a baby and then lull him to sleep. And then get him ready in the morning—be available at all hours.' I chuckle because she expresses it in quite a funny manner. Still, I can sense her grief. There is a proverb in Bangla, *Ghor achhe, bor nei*. One is keen to marry but cannot find a suitable match. Is it really that impossible for God to sculpt a life-mate for intellectual women? Rolda pulls out a wine bottle from her brown bag; we have purchased sandwiches on the way that taste of green Mediterranean chillies, twenty-five kunas each. We sit on the wide wall by the museum. A languid breeze picks up, charged lavishly with the perfume of foliage. I feel like humming a song. My nostrils fill with the fragrance of harad trees around Aamar Kutir in Shantiniketan. I sing Tagore's song for Rolda,

> '*Ami chini go chini tomare ogo bideshini. / tumi thako shindhupare ogo bideshini...Bhuban bhramia sheshe ami esechhi nutan deshe, / Ami atithi tomari dware ogo bideshini*'
>
> (O damsel from the alien shores, I know you. / You live across the seas...I have travelled the whole world to reach this new land, / I stand at your door, O damsel from the alien shores)

She does not understand a word but swings her legs to the tune. A golden swatch of the sun is glowing on her neck, her freckled, light-bronzed throat descends into an open-neck woollen blouse, the silk scarf on her neck is eager to take flight in the wind, but her small eyes are clenched shut. Her brown eyelashes, almost blonde, shiver lightly, the lipstick put on in the morning is flaked, and her hair is dishevelled, yet her face carries a rare calm. As if there is no hurry, as if she need not leave, as if there is not a single worry in this world, as if we have been sitting on this wall for ages; we don't have to go anywhere. The breeze, the sun, the strain of Tagore's song mingling with the wind—only these exist. She asks me to hum it again but instead of humming, I translate it into English. Suddenly Rolda jumps down, embraces me and breaking into tears, kisses me wildly. I am taken aback but I do not have the heart to push her away. Thank God Ivan is here. He teases us to lighten the mood. Rolda remains silent on the way back. I regret my song.

The car is moving towards Emina's house—I check the cells in the camera and the recorder without realising that these may not be used today. Ivan knocks on the door, Emina opens it—she appears much older than her real age. She is in a long frock flowing down to her heels. Bent at the waist, woollen socks on the feet, the skin on her hands is loose and wrinkled but her eyes are a startling white-blue. She must have been a rare beauty in her youth. We step into the sitting room. It bears signs of hardship—old, used things abound as if nothing new has entered this house for years. The walls are cracked and damp, there is a cabinet with steel wire mesh, and an old, uncouth, oblong fridge from a bygone age stands in the corner with a leg missing. In the tumbledown window frames, newspapers and rags have been stuffed in the cracks to stop the cold wind from entering. The wind has driven dry leaves and branches into a corner of the veranda. There is a lush cherry tree, and its boughs caress the door. The washbasin tap is broken and hanging loose, someone has tried to secure it with a piece of wire. The washbasin is rusted; it is hard to say how long it has been waiting for repairs. There is a long wooden desk covered with a Hrvatski newspaper. Dry pieces of bread, pickles, mustard, and sauce bottles lie on it. There is a brass samovar too—a rarity nowadays.

The curtain on the door is threadbare; it was probably brocaded years ago. Providentially, I have purchased a strawberry basket and two kilos of apples from Treg. I put everything on the wooden table but Emina glances at them indifferently.

There are no sparks of life in her extinguished, blue eyes. There is a photograph of her twins on the cornice, 'They are my only treasures. They are grown up now but I hardly see them. I feel terrified whenever I see them. I get goosebumps simply by remembering my disgrace and ill-treatment. The fact is, I am a prisoner of myself, unable to trust anyone. The fear still gnaws at me. There are a lot of people that lost their folks in the war, but they have managed to move on. I find it impossible. Probably because I was very young then. I keep asking myself all the time—why did this happen to me only? It is hard to disregard the past'. Emina reclines in the old, carved wooden armchair. It is the signal we ought to leave.

An NGO, Medica Zenica, looks after her, and she survives on its aid. Her health is poor and the monthly 170 dollar grant from the government is not sufficient even to cover her medical expenses. She has to take eighteen medicines every day for insomnia, back pain, depression, etc. She never goes out of her house alone. It was the government's duty to provide the necessary financial and psychological support to the war victims, but the Bosnian government failed miserably in the task. If women like Emina have survived, it is only because they came to Croatia. The assistance extended by the government was so scanty that the war victims were overcome by a sense of misery, of being cheated in their own land by their own government.

The women I came across in Zagreb have compelled me to mull over Bosnian women's plights too. I did not see Rolda after that eventful day, but we keep writing emails to each other. I have made an inquiry about Bosnia, and Rolda has sent a reply.

Dear Garry,

I'm sorry for what happened the other day. I don't know how you took it. I don't know you that well but since I love India, I like you too extremely. There is a murmur and softness in your voice that touched me when I heard Tagore's song, my favourite. In Europe, it is considered in bad taste to demonstrate one's anguish, pain, or suffering. You will see that people here try to conceal their penury and sorrow. Everyone harbours a similar grief but there is no one to share it with. Your country is quite different. I have seen women wailing without the tiniest hint of embarrassment, even men, beating their breasts to express their agony. In our country, we have a tradition of hiding tears even when we lose a close one. After the burial, tea, coffee, snacks, and wine are served to normalize things as quickly as possible. In your country, the last rites continue for thirteen days. There are so many ceremonies—from birth to death—endless celebrations when a child is born! How precious he is made to feel! I simply gape in amazement.

And now something important. The person working as a psychiatrist in Teufika Ibrahimefendich, connected to the biggest NGO in Bosnia, Viva Jene Tuzla, is my friend. For the last eighteen years, he has been treating war survivors suffering from posttraumatic stress disorder, anxiety, insomnia, depression, and hysteria. He has criticized the Bosnian Social Welfare Department by stating that in the entirety of Bosnia, there are 612 rape victims that receive the monthly compensation of 350 dollars each, but even for this measly sum, they have to manage medical certificates from a recognized NGO or government hospital every year. Often, they have to pay bribes. Those who fail, stop receiving the grant.

The Deputy Minister of the Human Rights Ministry of Bosnia, Saliha Dudreja, is aware of this downside of the government. He has confessed that the government has so far not succeeded in formulating a competent strategy to help war victims. The reason is the self-serving agenda of the political parties. A few prominent leaders of Serbia are still convinced that the Serbs never committed a wrong in Bosnia; moreover, war crimes against the Serbs have not even been taken up for hearing—it is tough to prove crimes like rape.

I will definitely write to you if I discover something. Drop in at my place someday. My granny has never seen an Indian. Please do.

Yours sincerely,

Rolda

***

Talking to Tomislav Maretic is like speaking to a crazy soul, he rants like a madman. He has a lot to reveal, yet he knows how to mask the shortcomings of his country. When I ask him about war victims, he starts talking about his haiku translations or moves on to the topics of Indian society and culture. Utterly fed up, I have informed Ivan that I will not come to the coffee house anymore as I am leaving for Bosnia.

***

The objective of the war against Croatia and Bosnia was to make the life of citizens so difficult that they would flee their villages, farmlands, and towns of their own accord. This would have facilitated the creation of Greater Serbia. The soldiers attacked citizens—mass killings, premeditated rapes, and concentration camps were part of a well-orchestrated strategy. During my vacation in the Priz Dor municipality of northeast Bosnia, I met certain men that were involved in coal mining, brick baking, and iron ore mining before the war. In the summer of 1992, Serbian soldiers gained control of the local administration and this huge stretch came under the sway of Serbia without the lightest military action. After this commenced the game of acrimony and savagery that left a mark of shame for all time to come.

The question vexes me—should one ever be pardoned for such heinous crimes? Jacques Derrida contends that forgiveness is a sign of weakness; there is nothing like forgiveness actually. It must be spontaneous, it should involve no conditions, and it should not be discriminatory. Communities considered civilised must examine the issues of retribution and clemency meticulously. After a crime is committed, the law can be used as an instrument to force the criminal to realise his misconduct, but once a punishment is meted there is little scope for forgiveness. It is a moot point—can a criminal ever be pardoned, a criminal who does not even confess his crime? Should the power of forgiveness lie with a non-actor organisation, an organisation that has never been a victim of this crime? If a woman's kid is slaughtered before her eyes, she should have the privilege of exercising the right to pardon, not the NGO fighting on her behalf. I agree with Derrida when he says that the right of exonerating the killer belongs only to the victim, not to an organisation. It often happens that religious and political leaders appeal for mercy publicly after a riot or an accident. They pay mere lip service; they do not actually regret the atrocities. It is a common scenario in our country, India. Hence, the contention endures—who should have the right to forgive and who should have the right to plead for forgiveness? Can individual loss ever be compensated by the clemency asked for publicly or by a third party? Even if an organisation takes up the issue on the victim's behalf, how would it assuage the sufferer's agony? It all boils down to the argument that the institutionalisation of amnesty is not appropriate—this right should be exercised only by the victim. We live through difficult times; it is almost hopeless to obtain evidence and eyewitnesses of such offences. Everyone must fend for themselves.

***

The questions plague me. In this part of Bosnia, I have come across at least twenty seven persons who have been searching for the bodies of war victims, their dear ones, even fifteen years after the war, in cemeteries, ditches, and foul-smelling marshes on riverbanks—casualties of mass murders. It is difficult to rub out the memories of the war. Sweto presented such an instance—a former soldier in the Bosnian army. When he saw a Serb in his shop, he asked for his name and shot him dead because he was the villain who had raped his sister. Such incidents are common despite the government's charade of amnesty. It is barbaric, however, it is an emotion-driven, individual act. My sympathies lie squarely with Sweto. Sad sagas of loathing and reprisal hang in the air even years after the conclusion of the war.

In 1993, around 20,000 Bosnian women fell sexual victims to the Serbs. Feminists such as Enloe, Otto, and Vance have analysed war in their own individual ways. Most of them believe that it is better to turn one's back on such incidents. Some even think that most of the sexual acts during the war were consensual. It hurts me deeply because I have met the women and their family members, those whose life was altered drastically by the war—thousands of women who lived through sexual violence were reduced eventually into commodities, enduring pain in suffocating silence. It is beyond doubt that mass rapes were used as a shrewd strategy. It had three objectives—first, instilling fear, second, coercing citizens to run, and third, rape as a reward for the troopers. Reagan Rolf has called the Serb army camps 'rape camps'. The International Criminal Tribunal for Former Yugoslavia conceded in the case of Bosnia-Croatia, that these were the first such cases in legal history. The credit for this must go to the doggedness of the feminist organisations that sexual violence was finally categorised as a crime against humanity—a war crime.

It was impossible for the victims to move on without consigning these dreadful incidents to oblivion. Astoundingly, such efforts were made earnestly by several women who digested the poison of their odious past to spare themselves ignominy, censure by the family, affronts to their dignity, and escape from the cumbersome legal process. This has prompted Jesmia Husnavoich, a researcher on Bosnian women, to declare—ignore your wounds, think about happiness and joy instead of pain, manoeuvre towards the dogma of optimism on the strength of your imagination and resourcefulness, and resurrect yourself as a redeemer in power politics. Nothing is bigger than life—not even suffering and painful memories.

The atrocities of the past cannot erase the present. A person merely needs a positive philosophy to live life well. Ceaseless tortures sink into history, trees with smashed roots blossom again. Survivors of war violence should be considered agents of social change. Still, how do we define a war? The more I view the countless cemeteries of Sarajevo, the stronger grows my conviction that war is nothing but an industry. Tragedies of war yield topics for conferences and workshops; a great deal of money is expended at national and international levels on the compilation of statistics and their analysis, and we learn about sites where mass murders and other barbaric acts were perpetrated. Spots like Kigali and Strebenise turn into popular tourist attractions. People eager to uncover the dark chapters of human history find battlegrounds expedient. Scholars conduct research on wars, and experts visit the sites and compose exhaustive but indecipherable reports. Such events also function as raw material for arts and literature. Karl Marx commented sardonically that crime is a necessary feature of society to fracture the inertia of the bourgeoisie. In a crimeless society, the profits reaped by forensic science centres, lawyers, judges, law digest publishers, and distributors shall disappear.

***

I wonder how it profits the victims, because during my search I realised that a couple of researchers consider even those women rape victims who never faced any sexual violence. There is a bizarre tendency to generalise, which assumes that all Bosnian women were raped. Had an attempt been made to study them as normal human beings, additional aspects of the war could have been analysed and traumatised citizens would have then found it easier to return to normalcy. The Croatian parliament resolved that women rape victims of the war would be awarded a one-time compensation of 100,000 kuna (around 14,504 dollars), 2,500 kuna every month, and life-long free medical and legal services. But it became possible only when the UN Security Council included rape in the category of war crimes in 2008, when thousands of such cases had come to light in Croatia's neighbouring country Bosnia, and in Rwanda.

Maria Sliskovic, the founder of Women in the Homeland War Civil Group, believes that this law will act as a guideline for the war victims of other countries too. There are diverse opinions on the amount of compensation. Ruzica Barbarik is sixty-five now. She was treated inhumanly during the raid by the Serb soldiers on Vukower in November 1991. She welcomes the government's decision but does not consider it a definitive solution. Snezna Malzaik, who has chosen to live in a small town on the Danube, is still awaiting government aid. Hopping through odd jobs, Snezna sounds exhausted, 'If I get the money, I can spend the rest of my life comfortably'. She says that she will not be happy as long as the culprits roam free. She wants to catch hold of them and ask how they were given a carte blanche to destroy the lives of guiltless women like her—women least bothered about political wrangling, women worried only about their families and farms. However, a handful of victims are pleased with the prospect of compensation. Zeba says, 'There was much delay but at least we have received something. Justice should be more than a mere word. I am sure this law will transform my life and I will not have to face further financial difficulties. The more I learn about such positive developments, the more I feel that I have come back to normal life. Women like us are considered human by the legal system once again, even if it has happened years later'. Another victim adds, 'Whatever the amount of compensation, it cannot really bring back what we lost; we want justice!' Even after two decades and several painful surgeries, Anna Horwantinek is unable to stop thinking about the inhuman assault, 'They were six. I was forced to watch what they did to my daughter and she was forced to watch what they did to me. My daughter died, but the trauma I underwent, who can repay it? I am consumed in the fire of revenge—an old woman, sick and alone—the criminals must be punished!'

***

The more I meet these women, the more restless I grow. True, ignorance is bliss. I sent a few pages of my journal to my friend, Nishaji, for a read-through. She too is distraught after going through them, but she advises me not to abandon my search midway. A friend from Thiruvananthapuram has communicated sadly, 'If we read this, we will not be able to continue a normal relationship with our wives'. Another friend, Shiba Aslam Fehmi, concurs that such happenings terribly upset one mentally and emotionally. What recourse do I have? Should I quit writing? Should I shut my eyes to this horrendous, traumatic chapter of the last century? Should I view only the skyscrapers, read verses only dealing with romance and joy, and delight at the enflamed clumps of roses blooming in the cemeteries of Sarajevo? Should I ignore that an innocent victim lies buried with all her unredeemed dreams at the roots of the rose shrubs? These were victims whose scanty bodily remains only could be salvaged by the relatives—maybe they identified some unfortunate victim through her broken skull. Should I take no notice of the storm raging in the hearts and eyes of the families conducting the burial ceremony with the customary last rites, no matter what, offering flowers at the tomb every Sunday? How can I?

***

I have stopped writing to my friends and relatives. Whom should I tell, and how—that my heart revolts against such inane formalities? I have promised myself that this week I will remain cheerful and pay no heed to war victims. What kind of life is this—*aye the haribhajan ko otan lage kapas*! (I came here to pray to God but I am picking cotton!) However, I am unable to escape my intuition, which senses the agony in every soul around me. I must get out of the house, meet people, talk, do something to connect, and reinvent the relevance of my existence to flee the bouts of depression. Most people do not recognise even themselves, their hollow laughter, pretended hurry, fake formalities, and absorption in cell phones and computer screens—man is not willing to countenance man. It is the grandest gift of capitalism. We are concerned only with ourselves, wading deeper into the pit of depression. In spite of the foreknowledge of the predictable reply of 'I am fine', we submit to the ritual of soliciting 'How are you?' Nobody has the time and capacity to unwind and bond. The moment we board a bus or tram, we push in earphones to avoid talking to others. The glow of life has fled with all its music; we have mislaid the art of savouring it. It is a universal curse, whether it is the West or our India. Commuting without interaction with co-travellers has become a sign of modernity. We are citizens with a state-of-the-art mindset!

Sprucing up the home, arranging books, folding clothes, gardening, etc. are chores that articulate our creative faculty, and yet these are not gender-specific, womanly chores. I suddenly remember my friends in Hyderabad and am gripped by a fervent urge to see Anupama, Boishali, Vasanti, and others.

I realise I must contact my friends in Zagreb too, life is turning sere without them. It has been a pretty long since I last invited Ivan, Kresho, Mirata, Bozac, and others to my place. When I arrived here from India, they helped me in every possible manner. I call Kresho—everyone else is keen to join. We fix a party this Saturday. My dear friend Guldane will not be able to make it because her sister from Turkey is here for a tour of Croatia. Since she can talk in English, I find it easier to interact with her. Still, I had no idea that the number of guests would swell so considerably merely at the mention of Indian dishes. Kresho's wife Sasha and Mirata too have joined us.

It has been pouring outside with a windstorm blowing since morning. I have donned several layers of clothes, topped with a long, deep green coat. My Indian shoes are useless here, the icy water seeps into them. I manage to come out to buy the foodstuff only after swaddling myself in this formidable armoury. A large variety of cheese is available in the shops. I purchase green vegetables, milk, and a ball of cheese; I already have some red wine. Kresho always says that red wine should first be boiled and cooled before consumption. It is used here as a substitute for water because it does not inebriate. It is beyond me to throw together anything more than cheese *parathas*, vegetables, *raita,* and salad. Dushka has baked the apple pie. In my opinion, the spread looks pretty appetising. I adore apple pies. She has trained me into preparing some. The cloves pinched in the pie remind me of the *laung lata* from Banaras. The succulent *laung lata* in sugary syrup, filled with *khoya*—it appears eons have passed since I tasted them last. Certain flavours hang back despite the passage of time.

The flat is very well kept and I feel like congratulating Elvira Mestrovic for her excellent taste. It is a two-room tenement—there are separate spaces for dining and sitting. There are large glass windows covered with curtains. We Indians are accustomed to white ambient light; here only the pale glow of the bulbs filters through the windows. I have requested the embassy to arrange white lamps in the reading room. Yellow light depresses me.

It is six in the evening and the guests have started coming in, in ones and twos. The house is filled with their gifts of flowers and chocolates. Andriana has come with Ivana as she is passionate about India and Indian food. Dining commences but Andriana's eyes are wandering. Ivana gestures to her. I am perplexed. People are talking loudly in Croatian and English. Since I am the host, I mind their plates. They too help themselves. Ivana goes out and returns with a large bottle; the wine multiplies their enjoyment. So, this was it! I had missed the drinks. The house is choking with smoke and the smell of whiskey. Mirata, Ivana, and I refrain. I find it quite strange. Sasha accompanies Ivana and Andriana, the chasteness of *parathas* has been defiled by the alcohol. They chatter nonstop; I feel nobody is in a hurry to return. The dinner stretches perennially. I am growing tired, there is some chagrin too. I need not have taken all this trouble. Andriana breaks into sobs, the others pacify her. Mirata declares that the moment she starts sipping wine, she begins to recall all her broken, shattered love affairs and unrequited trysts intensely. She goes on smoking and whimpering.

It is almost midnight. I drop the hint they should leave. It is pretty wet and cold outside, but Sasha has removed her coat. Even in her drunkenness, she does not forget to praise my dishes. My neighbour Dragitsa is still awake. The boisterous gaggle climbs down from the fifth floor. The '*dobrovechars*' (Good Nights) extend on for a half hour in the parking lot. It is almost one—I must tidy up the place and light a whole bundle of incense sticks.

***

As soon as the weather turns, the boughs shake off their snow sheaths. I don't see Mislav much these days because his classes run late in the evening. Moreover, he is a member of the Science Academy and is busy most of the time with his manipulations. Courteous and sombre, he does not have much of an idea about my work. Maybe most of the Indologists do not. He is the senior most, around sixty, and perhaps he does play a mean role in blocking the promotions of others—Kresho's innuendos suggest this much.

Professor Yeric Mislav has invited me home at lunch. His house is quite far but I enjoy the tram trip in the dazzling yet frigid sunlight. A couple at the tram station greets me with 'India' when they spot me in a *salwar* and *kameez.* I respond with a grin. Mislav's flat is in an enormous, ash-coloured building but there is no lift in this aged edifice. The broad staircase is timeworn. I count; it is sixty steps to the fifth floor; a good workout before dinner. There is a shoe stand to the left of the door, raincoats hang from the hooks. The door opens and I am welcomed with a warm smile. Mislav has just begotten a grandson and he has named him Sebastian. His daughter and son-in-law too are here. The garrulous son-in-law is a wiry graduate with thick glasses on his large, intense eyes. Mislav's daughter is standoffish; she is a prim example of European arrogance that has trained her into disliking the browns. Her fair, rotund face expresses a severe lack of interest; it is hard to trace a wisp of tenderness. Her body language divulges that she despises Indians. Mislav Yeric's wife Ivana is around sixty. She spent a couple of months in India a few years ago. The meal is plain but delicious. Dried potatoes, cake, salad, fritters—poor Ivana has prepared all the Indian recipes she knows. After dinner, Mislav talks about *Amarukshatak* which he is translating into Croatian. It was written by Amaruk in Sanskrit in the ninth century; it contains more than a hundred romantic couplets. However, he never shows his translation to any Indian scholar. I have often marked this tendency in Croatia. The authors are quite secretive about their Indology work with Indians because they realise that no Indian will ever read their Croatian renditions.

***

Last week, Yeric visited India to participate in a Sanskrit seminar in Tirupati. I had asked him to go to Hyderabad also. He is back now and has set up a photo exhibition of his India trip in the Philosophy Faculty. It is a singular experience for me—India through a foreigner's eyes—a sick, groaning, suffering India. The photographs were first-rate but the deliberate venture of projecting the country in a negative light was obvious. For instance, people defecating on railway lines, a cow whisking away flies from her wounds, the dense cobweb of cable and telephone wires in thickly populated settlements, the congested streets around Charminar, a pimp sort in a check print lungi—kohl adorning his eyes—at the mouth of the street, eunuchs dancing with saris flying, a middle-aged prostitute waiting for customers outside her shack, the betel spit soaked walls of Banaras University, close-ups of lepers and beggars at crossroads, damp walls of the guest-house in Tirupati, broken pails, pariah dogs gnawing at bones, an old beggar vomiting on the railway platform, the filthy slush on the banks of the Yamuna and the dim, dipping sun—I felt nauseous. Does this guy want to present this image of India to his students? The emerging middle class, broad, shiny boulevards, state-of-the-art airports, chubby, comely children of modern India, healthy, intellectual energetic youth, metro railways—he chose to ignore all these. There was not a single photograph that would tempt anyone to visit India. I found it impossible to stay any longer.

Later on, I shared my disgust with Kresho. He told me that Yeric still harbours the image of the old India in his heart. He is unwilling to see the new India—for him, it is still a country of sadhus, thugs, and snake charmers. We see only what we want to see. I know it is a personal choice, but I really feel bad, such pictures represent only one aspect of India or any other developing country. Possibly, they are displayed to project

India as an underdeveloped country—a regressive European attitude. I have my classes only three days a week this session. Yeric Mislav's research scholar too has joined, so it has taken a load off me. She has been to India several times and considers herself an expert on the country. Yeric Mislav listens to the erudite talks of his student almost in a trance. Kresho Kernitz teases him. He is translating Premchand's stories into Croatian. The teacher languishes—the student is going places!

The Tourism Department in Zagreb intends to publish a thirty-page booklet and I have been requested to translate it into Hindi. It takes me a week and I send the copies to Yeric and the Tourism Department. Kresho informs me with a titter on Sunday that Yeric and his research scholar are 'improving' the translation. I chuckle because I am aware of the depth of their Hindi—they are not beyond seeking the help of silly Google translations. I communicate my objections politely and decline to charge for my labour.

***

Writing a diary is a unique experience. It is like talking to oneself all the time. I do not know whether these pages will ever come to light but it has become part of my routine. To my amazement, I have transcribed my loneliness of the last summer vacation in the diary. *Ami hridayer katha balite byakul shudhailo na keha* (I am eager to pour my heart out, but alas, no one cares). Gradually, even this eagerness seems to have vanished. My folks back home too must be jaded by these sorry tales, but these are my only stories at present. Nadin Gordimer has called writing a kind of mourning that demands extreme isolation and introspection. We delude ourselves—*tomar katha hetha keha to bale na kare shudhu michhe kolahal* (No one talks about you here, they just make meaningless clatter). I remember my parents, but they are snug in their own lives. We must travel a lot to find material for writing but nobody other than the writer can tell what price he must pay for it. When the material is hoarded, he has to work on it alone. Rolland Barthes has called this self-contradiction of the lonely act of writing the signifier between the world and the people amid whom we exist. It is an act of endowing the best. Will I be able to deliver what I want to say? I am doubtful because my vision is blurred.

Hum zuban koi mile to usase sargoshi karoon
Varna behtar hai ki apni nazareing khamosh karoon.
I will open my heart only to a friend
Or else a hush in my eyes shall descend.

Sometimes I feel an intense loneliness, a pressing silence, and suddenly things become frighteningly strange and alien. My neighbour Dragitsa is a kind woman. She advises me to go to America if I want to earn money in the teaching profession. She has no idea how the Indian Council for Cultural Relations works. Had she known, I could have explained my assignment but I do not know enough Hrvatski. Finding me despondent, she plans an outing. She will take me to the bazaar for second-hand goods this Sunday. We have to catch bus number 295 from Zeprude station; it will carry us to Harelic market. The market is held on Sunday mornings, and by afternoon everyone leaves. We will have to get up pretty early. Since I am feeling low, I agree with the hope that the Sunday visit will usher in some novelty.

***

The Skype hour of my friends and associates is different from my time zone. When it is evening here, people are in bed in India. I sometimes feel my folks don't have much left to say. Anyway, there is Aryan, a security guard in the embassy; he is popular in Zagreb for his gentlemanly behaviour and knowledge of yoga. He is from Haryana and has great respect for teachers. He has told me about the facility of using the phone at very cheap rates. I can talk for hours. Nevertheless, vast geographical distances can make you gradually irrelevant to your native place without you realising when you are reduced merely to a silent spectator amid your own folks. There remain very few common platforms, moreover, the equation of fresh relationships casts you as a stranger. Earlier, I used to believe that Indians would never suffer the lonely fate of a Westerner, but the inhuman absurdity in the changing times and communities is forcing us into similar isolation. Even the closest relationships have begun to appear unfamiliar and artificial. You can only watch in utter helplessness. You are derided if you attempt to remove the walls. Emotions are vanishing—intellect and rationality are replacing them. There is obscurity and darkness, plucking out the ray of hope. The sentimental man is passé. There are no constant friends, no permanent enemies—*use* a relationship, this is how you traverse the enormous ocean of modern life.

Let me talk about someone who begot girl-children in India. Daughters can usually be cast into the oblivion of lost memories with the passage of time. There is pride in being a son's father, the heady pleasure of siring a male child in middle age is enough to erase the sins of the past. On the other hand, who was this woman, thirty-five years ago, one who forgot all her sorrows when she beheld her daughters reading and learning? Did not this ecstasy put out of her mind the fact that she, Debu Babu's daughter, never bore a son? She worked hard at making them excel in English and mathematics, even while she chopped *saag* on the platter or while shelling peas. She made us learn by rote the multiplication tables, forced us to finish our homework on desolate afternoons, to write essays—she taught us how to pray.

Three daughters at the callow age of thirty-two years and four months, the dream of a son wilting in Delhi's Kapoor Hospital, the dream of a woman who would hum tenderly, '*Tomarei koriyachhi jibaner dhruvtara, e samudre ar kabhu habo nako pathahara*' (I have marked you as my polestar, never shall I now stray in this sea of life)—the tune filled me with inimitable delight. I am proud that this learned woman in starched cotton saris, with the married woman's *sindoor* mark, goading us into studies—this slim-looking woman—is our mother! What wisdom she has, how expertly she cooks an assortment of dishes. She is Debu Babu's eldest offspring—so well-raised, so independent! Not even Debu Babu had the nerve to say 'no' to her.

I used to believe she would never cease to exist and that every morning we would wake up to her chants of '*namami shamishan nirvana roopam / vibhun vyapakam brahmaveda swaroopam / nijam nirgunam nirvikalpam niriham / chidakashamakashavasam bhaje aham / nirakaramonkara moolam turiyam / gira jnan gotitamisham girsisham*' (I bow to thee, Ishan, who exists in bliss / Who is omnipresent, who is the Brahman and the Veda / Without attributes, without replacement, without desire / You reside in our mind's sky, I worship thee / The formless core from where the sound OM originates / You are the knowledge beyond our knowledge, like the king of the mountains). Ah, the fragrance of the incense sticks! We would get ready, open the lid of the tiffin to see what delectables were in there and leave for school with a grin of satisfaction.

Didi would return with a bundle of complaints, Ma would feed us, and we would be reassured by her eyes that the world we had seen in the morning had not changed. Our dolls and toys, trees and plants, storybooks, chocolate and biscuit boxes, our beds, clothes, Ma's kohl-rimmed, meditative eyes, the broken nail on the middle finger of her right hand, the large round *sindoor tika* on the forehead—we exist because these exist, we are her polestar—*jetha ami jai nako, tumi prakashita thako, akul nayan jale dhalo go kirandhara* (Wherever I go, you burn as my polestar, let the stream of tears become a stream of light). The lilt of her humming lingers but she herself turned into a polestar one day, leaving behind her three disoriented daughters at an age when even sewing a button on the frock appeared a gargantuan task. Her polestars lolled in the dust, they had not even learnt how to cope with the future. We had simply gathered from Ma that reading books would lead us somewhere. The books became our screen to hide our streaming tears. We beheld her on each page of the book, spurring us to study. We treaded only on the road of academics. The eldest sister led through example. There were no friends, no kin; in the altered chemistry of the family, we had become outcasts. A sham financial crisis too reared up. It was books again that guided us like the polestar. We did not realise that walking this road would bequeath us nothing but books—*jabo kothay, jani na* (don't know which trail to take).

I feel as if all this had happened only yesterday—our shifting to our grandmother Ahilya after Ma's death. During the summer vacations, we soaked in grandma's doting fondness. Clad in a straight *pallu* sari, carrying a brass *lutiya*, we trailed behind her over the farm footways to propitiate Khudi Baba. Our life crop flourished as long as her petite, fair face, radiating the rich fragrance of *paan* and *zarda*, stayed with us. Nobody bothered about us after she passed away. Hopes wilted, Ahilya Devi and Debu Babu were gone. What remained was the scent of the red ants under the litchi trees, the mango, *karonda*, *biju* and *balbangra khiri*, clumps of *goolar* fruit, and the memory of the ominous-looking, towering palm trees in the murk of night at the back of our house. Remembrances…memories… iridescent images…Lord Satya Narayan's lore during his propitiation, Tara Rani Srivastava, *mamas* and *mausis*, Sunita's house, *tarbanna*, the dips in the canal, the rains during the

Ardra cusp, lentil-stuffed *puris, kheer* and mango feasts, the sharp, dusky features of Bari Mami, her shaking us awake late in the night to feed us…each scene comes alive. However, life moved on. Had I ever imagined that the home that endowed life and vitality upon us would remain unfrequented for such long years?

I start awake when Dragitsa calls. Hey, it is already morning! I often dream of my childhood, yearning to become the same old schoolgoing lassie, but right now I must leave. We travel in a bus to a large, grassy meadow. It reminds me of Tom Jones' song *Green-green grass of home*, which sings that a house surrounded by green grass does not require any other tint. There is the green grass and the railway tracks on a raised bank, and shops have been set up in a row in the middle of the field. It is quite different from other European markets I have seen so far. The sellers are men, women, and even kids. Most of them have laid their wares on the ground. Some of the goods are arranged on wooden tables. There are all sorts of pickles, chutneys, jams, and confections in arrays. They must have been produced at home as the simple packaging includes old, large and small bottles. Wearing scarves on the head, in long skirts, broad, freckled-faced white women are offering the merchandise at ridiculously low prices—decorative flowers and plants, a range of dry fruits, seeds, vinegar, cheese, eggs, dry meat, wild berries, craft tools, especially crochet table clothes and pillow covers. Their rates? Don't even ask—one-fourth of the market price! Dragitsa tells me that these folks assemble from the hamlets around to sell their produce every Sunday.

There are a number of toys spread on a rug, each is priced ten kuna (approximately 100 rupees)—old and washed out but usable. They have lost their usefulness in prosperous families and have turned up in the second-hand market. Not bad, at least a few children for whom life is nothing more than an accident, shall discover their childhood in the playthings. These kids are impatient to grow up—to earn two square meals a day and to get a roof over their heads. I see several middle and low class families haggling over prices. I purchase a teddy bear, I can't say why. Doesn't matter! It will sit in a chair, waiting for me to return from the university every day.

I lose Dragitsa in the bustle. Every face is white and most have put on caps to protect themselves from the sun. I glance around but she is nowhere to be seen. There is no signal on the cell phone. Panicky, I run around the carnivalesque flea market. Is she in the furniture section? Yes, there she is, in the midst of chairs, tables, and cabinets—old and new. Dragitsa is inspecting them, absorbed. I am relieved. I am always terrified of being lost. There is an assortment of tables, desks, and other pieces. Some look pretty ancient, maybe half a century old. Worn out chairs, the mark of the hands of the owner on the handles, intricately carved rosewood Victorian bedsteads—everything is absurdly cheap. I am astonished. Such lovely craftsmanship, with wooden poles in the shape of geese on four corners of the bedstead, dumb waiters, small stools, bookshelves with close-knit wire meshes—who were their previous owners? I am curious. How did such exquisite goods reach the market? Who considered these fine works of art so valueless? Dragitsa replies, 'They belong to *jivi saman*, persons living alone. Their owners are dead—*roba preminuo*—they passed away but their furniture has stayed back'. The huge mahogany armchair sways lightly—the invisible mark of the old hand with blue veins seems to be imprinted on it—as if someone unwinding in the chair has just risen to pull a volume from the bookshelf, leaving the *stolica* (chair) swinging.

One of the shops was selling almost an entire room—cabinets filled with books, paintings on the wall, a corner shelf. The books draw me. The shopkeeper intones, '*Ove knjige pristupachne, sizenna yedan kuna*' (one kuna for one book). Verse anthologies, dictionaries, novels, a book on music notations—the leaves are yellow and old but taken care of well, complete with a silk ribbon book marker. I caress the music notations and symbols as if someone else's touch lingers here. As if someone has just gotten up from reading the book and walked to the corner towards the three-legged old piano to play the notes; the fingers will glide awhile, and he will return to finish the composition. Someone will leaf through the book, lick the fingers and turn the leaves, a smile will light up as soon as the page is found, and then the book will be placed on the *clavir* (piano) book stand. The eyes will race over the notations and the fingers will jog on the eighty-eight keys of the grand piano divided into octaves.

The ebony keys are coming loose but as I run my fingers over them, I feel the long fingers of a great musician also stroking them. The concerto chimes from the high to the low—the rapture of the extinction of the self. Did the maestro experience it when he played the intermezzo? His fingers dancing on the flats and the sharps, plucking at strings in the connoisseur's heart—probably in the third *prahar* of the evening, when Raga Puria Dhanashree is performed, when damsel nature bashfully recognises her own splendour; or maybe in the last *prahar* of the night, serenading Raga Yaman with sonorous solemnity, thawing time and space. What a silly thought! It is the opera country, Indian ragas are not rendered here. Maybe the fingers waltzing on the keys were playing Mozart's famous Domine or maybe complementing the timbre of Zagreb's distinguished opera singer Mariana Radev. Or else, the virtuoso was drowning the self in a sonata, weary of the dismal, monotonous dirges of life. I ache to touch the grand piano, but not own it because a lot of his things, his fond purchases, have been forsaken here. The hour of the soloist is over; countless rhapsodies have been left untouched. Had his fingers kissed lovingly the keys before they moved off their cherished musical instrument? Did they tarry? Maybe he did not disclose to the nurse which allegro he wanted to play last. Maybe there was nobody around when the voice perished with its unrequited dreams.

Physically I am here, but the heart wanders. Dragitsa shakes me by the shoulder vigorously; I am embarrassed—what must she think! Anyway, why should we expect everyone to understand us? Such bonds are becoming rare. At the same time, I wonder if I will have the same luxury of free time in my country that I enjoy here.

***

Shahnaz's letter has arrived after long. I recall her sweet face. She had come to Hyderabad University for her PhD when I left Santiniketan. This quiet, beautiful girl, a student of the Hindi Department, was often at the receiving end of my rebukes. Bit by bit, she shed her timidity and started writing stories. Her father had compelled all his kids except her to study engineering because he wanted one child to stay with him. No sooner had she completed her studies than she was married off. I realise her misery of not being able to find a permanent post in any college so far. This girl is so fiercely independent that she never shares her feelings with anyone. And therefore, I must reply:

> Dear Shahnaz,
>
> I can very well understand the pangs of unemployment in spite of your degrees. I persuaded you to eke out a distinct identity. You have been such a dear student that your splintered voice and pauses on the phone have disclosed your unspoken stories to me. I have spent around ten months here but I do miss Santiniketan badly. Today is the first day of October. The wind is biting. There are violent gusts and squalls. The atmosphere is still and gloomy. The *kash* must have blossomed in Santiniketan, the drumbeats from the distant villages would have heralded the Durga Pujo. The rickshaw-puller at the Ratanpalli post office corner must be piping his flute in the evenings; the ashram would be enveloped in a mysterious, hazy cloak as soon as dusk falls. The *mela-math* trees must be preening their ears to the thumps and lilt of the *tablas* and the

tanpuras of music scholars practising in their houses. What time is it there? Probably eight in the evening; it is four in the afternoon here. Sometimes I wonder why I am here, in this alien land! How would it have mattered if I had not come here? I.A. Richards has spoken about aspiration-driven impulse. The desire to see and tour the world has dragged me here and all my official paths back to my own country are blocked until my assignment concludes. Even if we acquire the whole world, what is our true attainment? Man is not recognised nowadays for the sake of being human. The more you disconnect, the more postmodern you are! Even if one witnesses a murder, he denies it point blank. My stint at Hyderabad University has trained me in the new city attitude. Professionalism means being rude, discourteous formalities and silly, false smiles convert you gradually into something inhuman. Compared to that place, Santiniketan was rustic yet intimate—it preserved your humanity. In Zagreb, the bygone days knock on the door of the heart time and again, maybe because there is not much to do. Several Hindi professors occupying visiting chair positions in the neighbouring countries share their experiences with me. Most of them have made a trip to Switzerland. They have seen its dales and valleys with their own eyes while I have glimpsed them only in films. Posting pictures in tinted glasses and of snow-filled glens as if boasting, 'Look at my cushy fortune!' I too have learnt to pay lip service to their photos. This is the 'real' world, prodding you relentlessly into becoming a 'practical' person.

What should I say? Maybe, every path has its own obstacles. Since we cannot become corrupt, we must try for a job on the strength of our academic ability without being influenced by the wicked politics of complicity.

I observe here girls in different jobs walking alone on deserted streets in the thick of the night without any fear. No job is low for them. Families are small. Jobs are scarce but people are industrious. Until you get a lectureship, until your kids grow up, bolster yourself and immerse yourself in studies. You were working on 'Women's Role in Islam', what is the progress? Inform.

It is weird that the women here have suffered terribly yet they remain silent. We are enticed by their fair skin without comprehending the history of the conflict zones. I am collecting the narratives of quite a few of them. I don't know what I will do with them, but I jot it all down routinely in my journal. I will send certain portions, please go through them and express your opinion.

Take care.

Didi.

***

A banquet has been arranged in the embassy on Diwali. My house is pretty far from the embassy but Sasha has told me we can go together. The ambience at the party is quite formal; a number of India lovers, rather than Indian food lovers, have joined. The Ambassador's wife is amicable; she is also a good raconteur. Everything is stiffly ceremonial. The Indology people are hovering around the ambassador—the dark skinned ones, around the fair skinned—whatever one can grab! We return at five in the evening.

I learn at the party that the UN has arranged a meeting in Osijek to remove the post-war misgivings. Snezna is from Osijek, although she has been initiated by some guru in Kedarnath and has received an Indian name too; she is reserved and speaks little. I view the damage to nature and the dilapidated houses on the way to Osijek—it is not neat and ordered like Zagreb. The road is empty and desolate, there is nobody around. I have decided to stay here from Friday to Sunday. I want to write about the experiences of the common people in post-war conditions. Snezna's parents teach at a school in Osijek, and lead a frugal life. They remember the happenings during and after the war very well. Through the initiative of the UN, Serbs, Croatians, Bosnians, and Muslims were invited together to the meeting. Everybody was at a loss about how to break the ice. Snezna's father is there too, and his portrayal is so graphic that the scene that took place twelve years ago becomes alive, 'The participants are wary of revealing their names because the moment they do it will be obvious who they are—Serbs, Croatians, or Muslims. The moment they utter their names, their role in the war would be marked'.

Such meetings under the Building Sustainable Community in the Aftermath of War Project were held regularly by the International Rescue Committee between 1996 and 2001. The project received endowments from the UN Refugee Fund. Every year the forum met twice. The number of participants could be anywhere between sixty and ninety. These were the citizens that were social workers, doctors, nurses, teachers, and government officials in their respective countries and communities. The objective of the forum was to encourage mutual support and resolve security, health, and education related problems, and provide basic necessities in the post-war scenario. It sounded quite correct but the initial efforts met with little success. The memory of the torture was proving more frightening than the torture itself. Dialogue was next to impossible in groups of mixed ethnicities. The moment the war was mentioned, people became excitable or burst into invectives. They walked out of the meeting or assaulted members of the rival community. A firm strategy was the need of the hour, one that would orient them towards their problems and community-based creative development without hurting their war sores. If the border and civil disputes of the countries after the disintegration of Yugoslavia had been solved through talks, this easternmost part of Europe also could have been spared this horrendous violence.

In the beginning, very few people joined the forum. Those that did were old and sick, and the women were not willing to utter a word because they believed it was some sort of a trap. Ninety-nine per cent of the members sealed their lips whenever political issues came up, as if a dense sheet of fog had descended over them. If prodded, they would say, 'Don't talk about those days, the memories make us cry. Why should we expose our anguish? If we recount the tortures, the pain multiplies'. They were surprisingly against any political intervention in the meetings. They wanted social reconstruction but only through social efforts, not through a political option. They were men and women with experiences of the most vicious face of politics. The people in the meetings said that they could be considerate but the political leaders who wreaked havoc on their families and businesses and turned man against man, did not want to talk about them. After every meeting, they segregated visibly into Serb, Croatian, and Bosnian groups.

***

I had noted down my appointment with Fikret Ekik in the diary. I met him last in Bosnia; he was a jolly, sunny sort. Who could imagine that this fellow with the bird-nest-like auburn beard on his pallid face had lost his home and family in the war? He hid for months in the forest when the war began, satiating his hunger with tree leaves, licking dew in the rainforest. He traced his mother and brother when the war ended. His mother's state was abject. She trembled at the very thought of being ushered into a house surrounded by a boundary wall. Fikret decided he would rebuild his ancestral house. The house was constructed but it never became a home. His brother left one night in a fit of lunacy; he was later tracked to a mental asylum in Denmark. His mother too was put in the same hospital. What kept him alive after such appalling mishaps and his escape from the concentration camp? He replies, 'Because I can laugh, *smiyanzem me rupasiyo*, I am a person who laughs all the time. I survived because I laughed at my own silly jokes, jokes that generated sadness more than hilarity. Had I not learnt to laugh at my misery, I would have kicked the bucket'. Fikret is getting old toiling in his fields, but he relishes relating his tortures.

Most of the people from Prisedor in northwest Bosnia were occupied in jobs related to coal mines, brick kilns, minerals, and iron ore mines. In the summer of 1992, the Serb army controlled the local administration; the government did not come up with any martial response. Former Bosnia, suffused with the attar of labour and natural assets, went downhill, but the political leadership prospered and flourished.

***

I have also talked to Azar Blazevik and Edina Strikovic. They were detainees in the prison camp at Treno Paule for six months. When they were released, they bid farewell to the country forever. Edina was a child inmate in Omarska Camp. Later, she went to America for her studies, leaving one home to find another. She confesses, 'I'm still jumpy, I can't go back to Bosnia but I still remember it—the village, fields, crops, trees, my childhood neighbours. I want them to thrive in my memory so that I may tell the future Bosnian generation about the country's rich cultural heritage'. Her parents who were brutalised in the concentration camps still live in perpetual fear—they never feel at ease.

***

Dear Sergei,

I am coming across different women in the Balkan region. You were spot-on when you said that it is a person's inner strength that keeps one alive or kills him. Do you know? I met Yadranka, it was a unique experience talking to her. In fact, we met on the train and struck up a conversation. At first, I thought she was snobbish, but she gave me the address of her Zagreb flat and I visited her two days ago. It was a small flat with an open, tidy kitchen; the windows were overflowing with vines. Obviously, she is a nature lover. She is also a primary school teacher, a confident, independent woman—she lives alone self-assuredly. It was really good meeting her. A pretty, tall lady, she does not carry the baggage of self-pity like others. No one would believe that forty-eight-year-old, self-righteous, proud Yadranka was ever a rape victim. She served me boiled egg salad and green wine, then she pulled a chair, planted her hands on the table, and described her past in a detached manner as if she was speaking of some other person, 'At night, the soldiers would knock on the door and call us out. One night the Serbian commander Elko Mezavik summoned me. I was scared but I followed him into another room where there were already six or seven men. At first, he called me names and then ordered me to lie down on the bare floor. He sported with my body for four hours before I was sent home. I suppressed my groans and never told anyone; neither did anybody ask me. It was the unwritten law that women did not have to reveal what they had suffered'. During this torturous spell, Yadranka encountered Hasiba, a woman who had started loathing herself for the abuses and violence she had endured. Yadranka adds, 'I did not lose my self-respect after the rapes because for them, I was nothing but an inanimate object, not a human being. As a person, my dignity remained unscarred. Had I sold my body for bread, it would have devastated my self-esteem. It is self-confidence that gives you the strength to look into the eyes of the perpetrator, to show him that you know what he is doing. Physical force can hurt your body, not your sense of dignity'. She has preserved a picture of herself that was taken six months after the incident. It shows a young girl with luxuriant hair, piercing eyes, prominent cheekbones, and a face glowing with pride. She declares, 'I don't have any complaints against life, what happened is over. Many like me suffered a similar fate, why should I alone carry this burden?'

Everybody is not Yadranka. The sores on the body heal but the wounds inflicted on the heart remain green forever. Such hurts traumatise thousands of Croatian-Bosnian men, women, and children. Melissa, from Bosnia's Gorazad, still lugs undying memories of the blood-soaked last week of April in 1992, when ten to twelve women had concealed themselves in the basement with their babies, hungry and thirsty, waiting for the Serb troops to pass. In the dim light of a flickering candle they would tie cloths over the mouths of the kids to suppress any noise, any whimper that would disclose that they were hiding in this deep basement, starving and miserable. Still, they were not spared. The next-door Serb informed the soldiers and ten masked men jumped in. Hurling abuses at them, they snatched the feeding infants from the mothers' breasts. The neighbours might have concealed their faces but the voices were recognisable. They shoved the thirty-year-old Semsa into the room. Melissa knew Dragon K. and Bota J. very well but she had never imagined in her wildest dream that those who used to greet her with a polite '*Dobar Yutro*' (Good Morning) and lowered eyes, would undress her at knifepoint. Does the male species always wait for such a chance? The mask of gentility from the neighbour's face was gone, he thrust his phallus in Melissa's mouth—they wanted excitement! Melissa's mouth filled with an acrid taste, the corners of her lips broke. Another neighbour in a soldier's uniform kicked her in the waist as if spurring a horse. After the battering, she tried to reach her sister in Zagreb. It is the capital city, there must be the police and a government, 'perhaps I will be rescued', she thought, but the war was omnipresent. In fields and farms, in the hamlets, on roads, she kept hiding, often on an empty stomach. Sometimes she chewed leaves. When she threw up, she thought she was pregnant. She broke a tree limb and shoved it into her uterus to terminate the odious foetus.

In December 1992, she gave birth to a dead child in a Zagreb infirmary. She stayed at her sister's house but she never let her husband know what she had undergone, for she was afraid he would brand her wanton and drive her away. I do not know what to omit and what to note down. I have lost my sense of proportion after listening to these shocking narratives and transcribing them in the diary. Whenever I send a portion to you, the burden diminishes a little. Sometimes I feel I am exhuming the past but then I also feel it is a moral responsibility—my avowed destiny. I want you folks to read these pages of a history awash with blood and the tortures these women faced. I doubt they will hold the interest of any historian but at least my country should be familiar with them. Maybe the leaves of my journal will turn brown and dusty with the passage of time, without seeing the light of the day:

It is all raving. Please don't mind.

Hope to see you soon.

Best regards,

Yours,

Garry.

***

Enisa from Bosnia, who witnessed the murder of her father and grandfather at the tender age of sixteen, tried her best to hide and escape, but it was a futile struggle. Serb soldiers would barge into a house and rummage for cash, jewellery, and precious objects. They assaulted any and every woman. These soldiers were very well acquainted with the submissive nature of the inmates—pretty, delicate, innocent, religious-minded girls who had never thought before the war that being a woman could be a curse. They were intimidated and their jewellery and cash were snatched away to strip off their identity and self-respect. Enisa is thirty-seven but those horrible days of torment are still fresh in her memory like a movie, 'I took off my clothes when they threatened me. I was shaking in fear; something seemed to be creeping under my skin. I felt I was dying little by little. I was so young; I had not visited even the town by my village in Bosnia. My eyes were shut. He pushed me down and began the endless story of abuse. I lost my virginity, I broke down and cried but he was not moved. He stepped outside and called in two more soldiers. They repeated the torture. I lost consciousness; I don't know what they did to me. I don't know how long I lay alone in the pool of blood. I felt I had been deprived of my past, my present, my future; I was not sure if I was dead or alive. Is it the earth or the sky, am I awake or dreaming? Did this really happen to me? Is it simply a nightmare? I don't recall when mother came searching for me. There was not a string on my body. She broke into wails when she saw my horrid condition. I was naked, injured, and abused—Ma dressed me and hugged me. They had injured my vagina grievously. Mother washed it with warm water, sobbing, "*Zasto ste rodeni kao zena! Da umarieti ea umarieti!*" (Why were you born a woman? Die, girl, die!) Ma's stifled sobs brought home the bitter truth to me. I was merely a ruined body. Who will love me now? Who will caress me? Cuddle this broken, soiled body! All my dreams crumbled—my cherished wedding dreams! The boy who had loved me madly, did I have the courage to approach him now? I had no idea of the war, I had not once stepped out of my village. I felt my body was choking with filth. I was sinking into a bottomless gulf of self-pity. Why was I born? This body was ruined! My recollections of the trip to Trano Polzetak are muddled. The wounds suppurated; I found it hard to concentrate, wondering all the time why this had happened to me. I developed a cough and fever despite Ma's care and love. My body swelled. I adored kids. I loved their giggles, their glee, their lisps! But I shall never be a mother now. Doctors say I still have the infections—I am losing weight continuously, my immunity is failing. My mother is dead. I have no mate, no companion. In my world, man is a symbol of violence and revolting experiences. I hate every man; I am terrified of them. I cannot control this loathing!'

Women like Enisa suffer from post-traumatic stress disorder. Doctor Bozena Cook has helped several such victims. She believes that firm resolve is the greatest strength to tackle such situations. Occasional loss of sleep, avoiding people, remaining in a constant state of fear, nursing guilt feelings, seeking seclusion, and experiencing depression are the warning symptoms of mental disorders. If a victim of sexual abuse receives timely psychiatric help, she can return to normal life. However, it does not happen in most cases. Psychiatrists and counsellors did not visit the villages where such atrocities took place on a large scale, and rural women shied away from talking about their experiences openly. On the contrary, many victims in cities themselves contacted counsellors for advice. Bozena Cook says that one of the therapies is to tell the rape victims to record what they underwent and listen to it repeatedly. If the therapy continues for around a year, the sting abates. It is necessary to keep the victims occupied, to empathise with them, and to provide them with opportunities for supportive hearing. It seems a sound approach. If this could really be done, the victims would lead a normal life, but in most cases the families shut out such women, or else they suffer in silence, which affects their physical and mental health. Some found it impossible to readjust in marriage or moved out to faraway places to lead anonymous lives. A few committed suicide.

***

Classes are in full swing at Zagreb University. The campus bustles from eight in the morning till eight in the evening. The bubbly basement is called podrum, where there are a number of photocopy and coffee shops. Many university students work on an hourly basis in these shops. You can buy flower and fruit flavoured tea. I have almost forgotten the taste of our Indian milk tea. The air is filled with the aroma of baked coffee beans. You can find students and teachers at every table, sitting alone or in groups. You are lucky to get a seat. I also like to come here and write because I feel lonely and miserable in my flat. It is the perfect remedy for depression in a foreign country—meeting people. If you can't, park yourself at a spot where you catch life in full glory. Sometimes, I get the blues as I riffle through the pages of my journal. I am thankful that in my profession, reading and teaching work like healing.

***

It is July, and my neighbour Dragitsa has left to sunbathe on the Adriatic coast. There are thirty flats in the building but most of them are locked. The summer walks in with delightful harmony. When it departs, it leaves behind the gift of the showers. The sky is overcast; it is only three in the afternoon but it is already turning dark. The street lights are automatic. Darkness settles, lights click on, and exactly at this very moment, God knows why this raven-like bird perches on the lamppost by my window. The column is black and the lamp housing is moulded in Victorian fashion, emitting a pale glow. On a cloudy day, when the yellow light burns like a dim flame, I often notice this vigorous creature, around a foot and a half long, landing on the lamp post as soon as it turns on, as if waiting for the road to be lit. Its call is like the groan of a frail person who has seen a lot of violence, heartache, and pain in one's life—*creen-ee-ee*! Then it falls silent. It never comes with a mate. I intend to ask a student or Kresho what it is called. I should use my cell phone to click a picture.

The students are interested more in learning about India than learning Hindi—Madhuri Dixit's dance in *Devdas* and the amorous histrionics of Shah Rukh Khan and Hrithik Roshan. Valentina, in her third year, is friends with an engineering student in Maharashtra. They view each other online, share their joys and sorrows, and take dinner together before their laptop screens. Valentina has disclosed to me that she awaits 9 pm IST intently. She has set the alarm separately for summer and winter times on her mobile—in winter it is four-and-a-half hours behind IST, and in summer, three-and-a-half. Every night, she plops down before the screen with her food, on the dot at nine. Igor laughs as he informs me that Valentina never attends the Indology classes after six in the evening. It is her *dobrovechar* (Good Night) hour. I am curious about her Skype lover. Valentina reveals, 'We have never met, we chanced on each other on Facebook. He is handsome like a movie actor. He will get a job after finishing his studies. Maybe he will come to Croatia and then we might marry. He is dead against my going out with a Croatian boyfriend. We chat non-stop on the laptop or the cell, from dawn to dusk. I take up odd jobs on weekends. Every six months, I send money to him in dollars to pay his semester fees—he is a poor farmer's son. The drought has destroyed his crops. He has two sisters to marry off. He will come to Zagreb, and then we will live together'. There is a sense of deep commitment and adoration in the small, brown eyes, on the thin, oval face of Valentina. With her unwavering trust in this Indian boy, she pulls out the silver *bichiya* from her purse that she has bought in Barcelona. 'I wear them in the summer because they symbolise marriage in your country; however, it is uncomfortable in the winter, in the shoes.'

My suspicious heart melts at her gullibility. She saves a few kunas every weekend and then converts them into dollars at the end of the month. She visits Zagrebachka Bank every six months to transfer the money to an Indian bank. In distant Dharmabad, a village boy receives cash from the decrepit building of some cooperative bank. The conversion into rupee decides someone's destiny and success. What if he is unable to meet her expectations, or if he ignores her struggle? *My* standing will suffer. Doubts ricochet in my heart. I ask Valentina, 'Suppose his folks are not ready?' She replies, 'Then I will go to India. He will get a job or take up farming; I will look after the house'. Her trust, submission, and eagerness blunt my misgivings and prurience.

***

The dry leaves in Maximeer Park crunch under my feet. Valentina leads; the phone is glued to her ear. I somehow feel history is repeating itself—I have seen it somewhere before too. It is the feeling of déjà vu; scientists aver it is the sum of the memories stored in our brain.

This particular reminiscence concerns Sunadkishan from South Korea, who had joined Santiniketan to study Hindi literature but vanished suddenly. As course coordinator, it was my duty in the department to keep a tab on the foreign students. One fine morning, I learnt a startling fact about the girl following a police inquiry. Can I ever forget that distinct *Ashadh* afternoon in Santiniketan? The firmament was azure following the morning downpour. The emerald paddy crops, in the brilliant sunlight, appeared sunnier. The trees and the shrubs looked fresh after the shower; the red soil had drunk water copiously to match the dampness in the air. Ants were scurrying down the palm trees, lured reckless by the heady scent of the jackfruit bursting with ripeness.

Worker ants were intent on carrying the sweet seeds. The biggest, lowermost leaf on the palm branch, unable to bear its weight, was hanging half-broken, almost coming off. Sweet-smelling clumps of the spring *malati* blossoms were still dripping moisture and in this picturesque background, a feminine figure with a tonsured head emerged in a yellow sari draped in Bengali fashion.

I found it difficult to believe that this girl was the only heir of her millionaire, mountaineering parents in Korea. A surfeit of luxury awaited her homecoming in South Korea but she has taken to the life of a *baul* now. Her *baul* guru in Rangamati has revealed the path of self-realisation to her. She is reluctant to own her opulent past. I was moved utterly when she wrapped the *anchal* around her neck and sat on the ground to greet me. What blessings could I offer? Extricate yourself from your guru's snare; come, hold my hand and I will lead you back to your own folks! Maybe I should have told her to have complete faith in her guru if her love was true. And then she crooned the Bangla number sung at Tagore's Jorasanko house in 1921—she had learnt it in the last six months. What was left for me to say?

Aji jharer rate tomar abhisar
Paran sakha bandhu he amar
…
Sudur kon nadir pare, gahan kon baner dhare

Gabhir kon andhakare hatechho tumi paar
Paran sakha bandhu he amar
(This tempestuous night is the time for your rendezvous,
O my soulmate, O my friend.
...
On the bank of some distant river, through some dense forest
You are crossing the deepest darkness
O my soulmate, O my friend.)

I am unable to put out of my mind the poignant tune of her lovelorn ditty; she sang it in a trance, her eyes shut, even if her Bangla accent was imperfect. Had she really found her soul mate—one for whom she had passed through the stormy night to Bolpur, to sleep on the ground, to fix his marijuana chillam, and pass it to his greasy fingers? She had sacrificed everything to win the accompaniment of the guru's *ektara* to her song, bowing at his grimy feet with cracked, overgrown, dirt filled toenails, dressed in his umber clothes, lounging within his reed hut. It is difficult to reckon how long her devotion for steadfast service to guru, her zeal for cooking *machh-bhat* on the earthen oven, and her ignoring all impediments as a swain after landing in his house on a thundery, murky night, will hold up. It was my last meeting with her. I get a similar feeling when I look at Valentina. I want to hold her by the arm, to caution her—emotions make a woman strong and emotions make a woman weak. She submits her whole being in love, attending to the smallest need of her beau. Her overflowing love transfigures into doting care. If her man is worthy of containing this concern, he attains ennoblement, failing which the woman turns into a hostage to her own self. She bears the joys and sorrows, possessions and patronage of her man, owns his passion as well as defects, but the unscrupulous man cuts and runs, branding her a sentimental gull. Impulses of youth reduce a woman into a readily available commodity. By the time she realises it, her love slips away. It cannot ever be wished back again in its prime, pristine form. I want to warn her, 'Don't confuse money and love because money breeds avarice, not tenderness. A woman must weigh the pros and cons before falling in love'. However, I desist—Valentina might be offended.

***

I always get the blues in my birth month, *Sravan*. My grandmother tells me that the skies had opened up the year I was born. Tehsildar Babu's elder brother, Jagnarain, was pensioned off ahead of time when the Pachrukhi Sugar Mill downed shutters all of a sudden. His passion for football and Kabir was next only to his love for meat and wine. He was familiar with all edible creatures in the water, sky, and on land. He never missed a chance to narrate self-importantly his nostalgic recollection of being selected to the football team of the whites, how he spoke English fluently, and of stumbling back home late at night, singing at the top of his voice a sardonic solo, wishing a happy conjugal life to the middle brother Nag Narain.

Nag Narain bade angna, dekh tare kangna

Hum bani duara, dekh tani puara.
(Nag Narain frolics with his bride, amorous and gay,
I stand forsaken, counting bales of hay.)

The bizarre song echoed far in the stillness of the night. The dog lounging coiled up in the snug warmth of the hay would stir, shake its body, and commence barking. Jag Narain Babu's tubby, newlywed, youthful wife would jump out of the bed with a start—her protruding teeth could not be contained within her thick, full lips, always jutting out—drape the anchal over her head, and unlatch the door for her *jeth* resentfully. As soon as the doors opened, all the feline and canine beings in the neighbourhood would rush in with Babu Sahib into the courtyard, where rice gone cold and *sagauti* would lay covered in an aluminium pot. The cats would gaze patiently at Babu Ram Narain Prasad partaking of his supper. The dogs lolled out their tongues excitedly, swallowing saliva in the hope of getting hold of the leftover meat or fish. The entertainer would eat a bit and toss the remainder to the waiting horde. Srikanti Chachi used to say, 'Since Babuji fed mostly the cats, he never had his own sons'.

Whatever the reason, it was true that he spent all his time at the local saint Alkanand's monastery, singing *Kabiraha* and smoking pot. The *maat* was surrounded by mud apple trees, cool and shady. Years passed but no brass saucer banging heralded childbirth in the younger brother's house. The responsibility of carrying on the family line fell on the shoulders of the eldest son. The moment the news of the birth of the granddaughter spread, the elder brother started dispensing the so-called charmed ash from the *maat* to his wife. She, although educated, would sometimes disregard her education to consume the ash within her veil and sometimes chuck it on the sly into the drain. The pot smoking saints had guaranteed the birth of a grandson; it was to be followed by a huge feast! However, what can a mortal do if Destiny dissents? She finally begot a child, but it was a daughter once again—the gloomy news, received on a postcard during the soggy days of thunder and copious rains, posted on a date that coincided with the birthday of Nelson Mandela, drove him to the bench patronised by heartbroken souls in the local toddy bar. He broke into a bawl, hiccupping, tears rolling down his cheeks, nibbling the *chakna* with the hooch, '*Ka ho Ram ji, kahan sootal bani*?'—O Lord Rama, why have you abandoned me?' The louder he wailed, the more commiserations he received, but most of the gestures were motivated by sated jealousy and envy. It would have been a surprise if people were not resentful of his property and his prosperous farming, joined with the money-spinning post of the *tehsildar* in the Saharsa Kutchery. I don't know why, but having heard this tale over and over again since childhood, I developed an inordinate grit to prove myself. My paternal cousin Rahul Bhaiya, Kajal, Chacha Vikas, Neeraj—I held everyone as a competitor. They were supposed to be the 'Light of the Dynasty' and I, a paltry girl, of no value! We never can outrun our sentiments and attitudes, no matter where we go.

***

Today I am remembering Santiniketan, an abode where I beheld and felt nature up close. Who in the concrete jungle of Delhi has the leisure of gazing at the undesirable, grimy, groaning trees strangulated by steel wires? Santiniketan's greenery, its natural beauty, pulls one to itself. One of my favourite pastimes was driving my scooter on the road along the Kopai River, racing with the train chugging to Malda. Manju Rani Singh spent a lifetime in Santiniketan—her learning, her jobs, everything. She would point out the trees and plants as we walked along the footpath. I have been intending to write to her. She is uncomfortable with emails so I will send the letter by the weekly embassy post. A letter must be mailed to Doctor Chandrakala Pandey also—a globe-trotter! Leading a lonesome yet dignified and independent life, she is quite fond of me. She has had a long political career; I feel like asking her to write her autobiography—she has not been able to muster the courage to write it, even after turning seventy. I can never write regularly and I seldom feel like reading my journal. If I do it inadvertently, it drains me. I have transcribed the stories of several women. As many tales as their lives—every life a narrative—filled with histories. A victim cannot turn a blind eye to one's wounds. Remembering itself becomes an act of pain. Come on! Why should one recall the atrocities, we live but once! If a dream shatters, the rest of our life is spent picking up the shards. For the listener, these experiences are but mere prattle. A whole class of European women are eager to relive life despite their great torment. It may sound admirable. However, I will narrate their horrific accounts for those that will inherit the future, for those who dream of visiting a charming, perfect Europe.

Dear Chandra Madam,

After landing here you are one of the people I keep thinking about. I came last December. I had thought I would write to you only after settling down fully, so the delay.

There is not much to occupy me in the department. If I go on using English in the class, I may forget how to teach in Hindi once I return to India. I am learning Croatian from my students. I have learnt the digits—*jedan, dva, tri*. I even understand a little Croatian now. I have met all sorts of people here but all that when I see you next. However, I had not the slightest idea in which deep woods of Europe I would discover my stories. How could I? We are so terribly engaged in the inland politics and matters of our own country that any news from distant Europe appears strange. It is only when we run into them that we realise how petty our own concerns are. Sometimes it is the other way around, especially when overindulging in intimacy obstructs our vision. Tagore has written:

Bahu din dhare bahu krosh dure
Bahu byay kare, bahu desh ghure
Dekhite giyachhi parbatmala,
dekhite giyachhi sindhu.
Dekha hoy nai chakshu melia
Ghar hote shudhu dui pa felia
Ekti dhaner shisher upare

Ekti shishir bindu.
(I have travelled thousands of miles through numerous years, spent a fortune travelling to faraway countries, and beheld mountains and the oceans, but I failed to see the dew drop on the tip of a rice blade close to my house.)

As I look at things from this perspective, the vision of countless ignominies suffered by Indian-Asian women during the Bangladesh freedom struggle revives. Whenever I taught the stories based on the Partition of India and Pakistan, for example, *Sharandata*, *Khol Do*, and *Thanda Gosht*, I used to believe it was merely a spent past. A fiction. I was only supposed to discuss their theme and technique academically. However, the narratives I am confronted with, of these broken women, masking their grief under layers of mental veils, reawaken the characters created by Manto and Ajneya. I hear stories in Croatia and think about my own country. The space of thousands of miles vanishes—it is the universal human fate. Whatever the setting or structure, the stories I had read but never identified with, have become alive. Manto's Sakina breathes when I talk to Enisa—Sakina cut off from her family, reduced to a body only. Enisa is Sakina, Sakina is Enisa—she understands only the words *khol do* ('Open it'—a command that meant to her, 'untie the strings of your *salwar*') in the haze of her fainting consciousness.

'For a while, he stood numbly against the wooden pole outside the hospital. Then he walked inside listlessly. The room was bare. There was just a stretcher, a corpse lay on it. Sirajuddin stepped hesitantly towards the dead body. Suddenly the room was filled with light. He caught sight of the black mole on the pasty face of the body and cried out "Sakina!"

The doctor, who had switched on the light, asked Sirajuddin, "What's the matter?"

Sirajuddin managed to whisper, "Sir, sir…I…I'm her father."

The doctor felt her pulse and pointed towards the window, "Open it."

Sakina's limp body stirred. With lifeless hands, she untied the string of her salwar and slid it down. The old man, Sirajuddin, shouted in joy, "She is alive—my daughter is alive!"'

Similarly, when I was reading Yashpal's *Jhootha-Sach*, I thought that it was a historical novel, fictional. But I see it's Tara in Dushka. When Dushka parted from her boyfriend, her life crashed. Yashpal's Tara lost her lover because she was a Hindu. She was denied a sense of security even in marriage.

'She is a Hindu. Why shouldn't we defile her? These shameless Hindu girls are fit only for this treatment.'

'What if the Hindus say the same thing about you? A woman should understand another woman's pain.

God forbid you suffer this fate. Allah-ta-ala has created differences between Hindu and Muslim men, not between women.'

'These scamps fight each other but it is the women that suffer.'

'The Almighty Lord has given man the duty of looking after women and taking pity on them because it is a woman who gives birth to man and raises him.'

'Pity and care, my foot! These rascals defile the slits from which they emerge. Whether they love us or are wrath with us, it is the twat they ravage.'

You must be wondering at my jabber. When do you intend to begin your memoirs? Hindi literature is poor in autobiographies of women with political careers. It is time you started. At your age, you needn't bother with how others will react, do what you think is right. In our culture, women neglect themselves pitifully to keep others happy. I feel good when I see women of your age here getting the finest make-up, donning the latest dresses, making friends, singing, dancing, and enjoying wild parties. Some of them are real devil-may-care dames; they don't even let out that they have grandchildren! They live for themselves—rising above pettiness to enjoy the world. And look at us! We waste most of our time grimly preparing for the afterworld, incapable of relinquishing our weakness for sons, daughters-in-law, and grandchildren. We revel in our serfdom, in our families. You have led a productive life, you are well-read, and you can recount your countless conflicts in your autobiography—our generation has a right to know. I repeat, renounce self-denial and let the world go to hell! The bitter fact is that nobody is concerned about a woman's intellectual and creative side; most of the critics are interested only in counting the skeletons in her cupboard. Despite constraints, women like you must be daring enough to record their autobiographies.

Warm regards,

Yours,

Garima.

***

The three-and-a-half-month university vacation has started. Like many other teachers from other countries, if I want, I can return to India and come back when the session begins. The Philosophy Department at Zagreb University is deserted; the crowd of students, the laughter, and the banters are gone. I can hear the bang of my own boots in the corridor. Some of the teachers are occupied quietly with studies in their chambers. The rooms are clean and comfortable. Central air conditioning maintains the warmth inside. The professors study till late at night. The vagaries of the weather outside do not disturb their work much. White blossoms are in full glory—here are tiny, countless flowers on barbed branches, exquisite velvet-like petals sans fragrance. I recall the concluding lines of Wordsworth's *Daffodils*,

For oft, when on my couch I lie
In vacant or in pensive mood,
They flash upon that inward eye
Which is the bliss of solitude;
And then my heart with pleasure fills,
And dances with the daffodils.

***

Dora Mikhovic is a professor in the English Department. I often see her in her chamber, lost in her studies. Guldane has introduced me to this elderly lady but we are not close. Her voice is raspy yet she looks vigorous. Guldane tells me that the war has scarred her too. I ask incredulously, 'Was she also…?'

'Oh, no! She lived in a posh locality of Zagreb. Wife of a high-ranking military officer.'

'What actually happened?' I probe.

Guldane does not reveal much. She is learning Croatian so she often talks with Dora. Dora seems to like me and we converse in English almost every day, however, she never speaks about her private life. She teaches Shakespeare and Milton, and her acquaintance with India through books is sound; she has also read the Vedas and the commentaries on the Upanishads. She believes that Indians are religious, irrational, and penurious. When we go for coffee together, she pays for hers promptly. Her gesture makes me uncomfortable and I have begun paying for her coffee too. She accepts with reticence. She gazes tenderly at me but never asks about my life, although we sit together for hours. We discuss languages and literature but her shield of reserve does not budge. One day she brought some walnut wine. This traditional Croatian wine is made by grinding together chunks of the raw walnut fruit, *orahawok*, with orange and lime leaves, blended in red wine or vodka and left to ferment for forty days. Wine is made from different kinds of fruit in every home. Walnut wine is supposed to be a special gift. It is taken in glass shots. The deep brown liquid is poured in squat, lovely crystal tumblers, like those used for dispensing homoeopathic doses. A cake covered in dry fruit is placed in the middle of the table. Gul finally announces that it is the birthday of Nisa, Dora's daughter. Ten-odd people are attending the party. The walnut wine is admired generously; Dora puckers her painted lips to attest to the wine's antiquity. The shot burns my throat. *Nah*…it is impossible to swallow! Everyone chuckles.

***

I decide to visit Nisa. Tall, slim, with short brown hair, uncaring for her femininity, I doubt she has ever used makeup. Her hands are long and coarse as if they are used only for labour; they do not need any attention. Her lips are chapped. There is a weird hurriedness in her sentences and actions. She does not sit in the chair cross-legged like other women but with legs apart, recklessly, in a small check shirt and washed out, torn jeans. Her knowledge of world geography and history is considerable; she is quite unlike Dora. She and a friend of hers have adopted a child. Her girlfriend is physically challenged—she is a paraplegic. The three-year-old kid is holding Nisa's finger. She walks up to us, pushing her wheelchair.

She is not reluctant to tell us about her past. What is there to hide after all the abuses she has suffered?

It was 1992, May 15. The Serb soldiers knotted their stinking socks over Nisa's eyes. The miasma assaulted her nostrils, throat, and lungs. She snatched them away in revulsion and alarm. Then they whipped her until she yelled, 'Serb socks don't smell!' They raped and pounded her relentlessly. When she fainted, she was doused with ice water and they hit her face with rifle butts to jab her back into consciousness. The soldiers wanted to extract information about the army officers so it was vital to keep her awake. Nisa pretended insanity to evade the torture. She would bellow Serb songs in an ear-splitting voice, dance berserk, tumble deliberately into the lap of the cruellest and most violent soldier, and light the cigarette in his fingers. He would use the burning tip in wicked ways on her body. Her heart hissed, 'I'll break out!' despite the innumerable wounds she received on her body and soul. Her bouts of madness, giggles in the harshest moments, her wild bop with lifted skirts, her dishevelled hair, and sipping dregs from wine bottles finally persuaded the Serb soldiers that she had gone nuts. It was futile to ask her about the army general. Restrictions were relaxed, her tormentors shooed her away. Finally, one day, she concealed herself in a potato sack and fled the concentration camp in a ration truck.

She was an educated woman; she assumed a new role in Vienna and scripted heartrending tales about the brutalising of women, children, and men. Of kids that had witnessed the rape of their mothers and sisters, and the gory spectacle of their brothers and fathers being shot in the head. They had watched how prisoners were forced to lie naked on ice blocks for hours. The soldiers flogged the menfolk, raped the women, and took out their intestines to strap their hands and feet, leaving them writhing in puddles of blood and agony. The kids also witnessed the studied, stony silence of the Serb neighbours. Crying in endless pain, many children died. Nisa noted two resolutions in her diary. First, she would devote her entire life to the rehabilitation of such children; second, she would never marry. I don't know what to say to Nisa, my heart has turned moist—*nibhrita e chitta majhe nimeshe-nimeshe baje, jagter taranga aghat* (In this desolate heart, the ache of world's misery rings in every fibre). I have lost my peace of mind. I had a peep into her soul and now I feel as if she is an old, intimate friend. I remember Muktibodh,

I belong to them
Those from whom I have received this form and sentiment.
They are close to my heart;
Those who bore on my life.
They own my words and my sentiments
The feet and my path too
My end and meaning too

The attitudes are theirs.
I walk higher and higher
Through their lowliness
It is their shallowness
That makes me so deep.

***

Seda Branich is Nisa's friend. She was born in Travnik in Bosnia in 1949, studied in Zagreb, and joined the Belgrade daily *Borba*. She arrived in Geneva as a refugee in 1992. She tells me that in 1993 she had come across a woman who had suffered atrocities at the hands of the Serb soldiers but had managed to escape somehow with her two kids. She had blubbered with great effort, 'They're slitting throats, killing, setting fire to people in their houses, raping!' The moment someone asked her, her coagulated pain thawed out in streams of tears. Her terrified eyes revealed to me the horror of rape. Hungry and afraid, shielding her son and daughter from the cold, spending all her savings to attempt a border crossing, no one knows where the woman finally vanished.

Seda visited several refugee camps in 1993 and 1994 and met many Bosnian Muslims in the Folnegowic refugee camp near Zagreb.

***

I can talk to Nisa and Seda through Dora but there

is something else that prompts me to dig deeper into the background of the war victims; sometimes the same urge also holds me back. However, untimely rains have brought on the throat infection once again. I find it difficult to swallow—here you can't get medicines over the counter as in India, you must have a prescription. Sucking on cloves has left a bitter taste in the mouth. I sound hoarse but I am so exhausted that I don't feel like going to the doctor's. Such lesser sicknesses take a toll on time. To escape it, I must jot down what I feel without wasting a second. Nobody can predict the future. Sometimes I feel I have known this country for years, often it turns so very strange. The ground that I walk upon has witnessed the spilling of blood of countless innocent men and women—spots where dreams wilted into nightmares.

The route I take in the evening is flanked by rows of large, bloodshot rose blossoms. I notice that they have not withered even after days. Since it is not my own nation, I am chary of touching them, still, I gather courage and stroke a flushed one—stout, velvet petals, the buds too are robust and fleshy. I raise it up to my nose…there is no smell…no fragrance. The soul of this nation too seems to have lost its perfume and essence. The mothers, sisters, and daughters that were raped, battered, and tortured in every house, appear normal outwardly—healthy and composed—yet their core history is one of blood-spattered, tormented, anguished evacuees. Unless we confront such circumstances personally, we cannot truly comprehend the meaning of words like 'violence' and 'sexual abuse'. This evening, as I am noting down the statements of women buried under bizarre stenches and unarticulated cries, the words of Siada Wravich echo in my ears, 'Before I met the war rape victims, I used to believe that rape is a man's psychopathic aberration. An attack—the target is the woman's genitalia—an act still sensationalised in print and electronic media. Breaking news! A deed about which funny excuses are furnished—the perpetrator was unable to control himself or that a particular dress provoked him! It is also rationalised as man's natural instinct. However, I have come to the conclusion that it is not man's sexual impulse but his fear of death. Such attacks are never made for the sake of self-defence. There is not a single instance to prove that a man raped a woman simply because the woman had assaulted him first. The wounds are invisible but mortal. A most effective weapon that lacerates the heart as well as the mind; the injuries are so deep that the molested, helpless victim cannot even articulate it fully.'

The statements and data collected after the 1995 war by voluntary organisations, governments, and western feminist organisations in the villages presented shocking and contradictory reports. In the Zenika region of Bosnia, on average, one complaint was reported every twenty-four hours, while the rate was lower in the cities. The fact was that only one out of ten cases was reported. The Bosnian government reported 50,000 rapes; Zwonimir Seprovich (who works for war victims) believed it was 30,000. The European Union investigation committee claimed that it was 20,000.

***

I see not the numbers but women. One Bosnian family's menfolk ran into the forests to escape but the mother and the daughter were caught and raped relentlessly for a month. Still, the women never let the men find out about their abuse. In many families, the women hid their brutal persecution from their men. They tended livestock and the farms with tormented hearts and bodies, waiting for their men that had gone to the battlefront as soldiers, or had been taken prisoners in concentration camps. They went into hiding, never to return. Whose daughters and mothers were they supposed to be now?

As far as the Bosnian Muslims are concerned, they are fundamentalists like in other patriarchal communities when it comes to women's virginity. If they have the slightest suspicion or evidence, they do not think twice about divorcing the spouse. In the United Yugoslavian law, sexual violence unleashed on a wife was not considered a crime. Thousands of Bosnian women did not report their sexual abuse out of the fear of ostracism or for the ignominy of remaining spinsters or divorcees. I talk to a woman who did not have the nerve to inform her husband about the evildoing of her Serb neighbour. Even after the war, she was afraid to ask her husband, who had returned from the front, to shift houses, although she was badly terrified of the wicked grins and filthy, furtive gestures of the neighbour. Just like India. In our country too, women are powerless to reveal their sufferings.

***

Incredibly, not only women but men and children too fell victim to inhuman sexual viciousness. They were forced into sodomy in military camps. Ivan informs me that starving, naked, wasted captives were forced to have sex with other male prisoners. The acts were photographed at gunpoint. It was a shrewd strategy towards the formation of Greater Serbia—tipping off the international media that the Bosnian-Croatians are racially depraved. What should I acknowledge, and what should I inscribe? Doubts stymie me; sometimes I really believe that ignorance is bliss. Like other conventional tourists my trip too could have been exciting, cosy, and street smart. People could have seen through my eyes the natural beauty of this part of Eastern Europe—the emerald, crystalline sea, the boundless stretch of archipelagos, the ancient Roman architecture and so much more! However, it never happened. My sight is crushed by the past of this place and the thousands of mute but indefatigable women. Yesterday I noticed the petals of the velvety rose had fallen; the reedy, spiky twigs too are withering. The dry bud poised on top of the stem may topple at any moment. Dora advises me to read *The House of the Good Neighbour*, a volume based on the experiences of the First World War. Its author, Esther Pohl Lovejoy, was a medic. She has discussed the health conditions of common citizens during 1917-18, especially women and children. Thousands of women had to obey the soldiers and disrobe. Women that became pregnant had no facilities for abortion. As soon as the news of a pregnancy spread in the camp, the soldiers would begin celebrating with songs, dances, and wine. The war spawned thousands of orphans.

The far-reaching consequences of the Second World War had already set in motion the Croatia-Bosnia conflict during 1939-45 when the United States of America and Soviet Russia were in a state of cold war. Countries around the world were divided into two camps—the socialists under the leadership of Soviet Russia, and the capitalist nations under America. They remained in constant dispute—the Berlin Crisis, the Korean War, nuclear explosions by Soviet Russia, the Sino-Indian conflict, the Cuba Missile Crisis—all these had resulted from the cold war. The Eastern European nations joined the Soviet camp and formed a military organisation under the Warsaw Pact. The twelve countries with America founded NATO. Significant changes followed on the international skyline.

Eventually, a growing fascination for capitalism became the chief cause behind the disintegration of Soviet Russia. In most of the communist countries too, the clamour for democracy was on the rise. It was also the period when United Yugoslavia was deleteriously affected by the events in Poland and Romania. With Russian power on the wane, the stage was resolutely set for the disintegration of Yugoslavia. Tito's absence brought in a radical reversal. People create history through their encounters. Croatians, Bosnians, and Herzegovinians, least bothered about the affairs between Russia and America, loath Slobodan Milosevic today. People construct history through their involvement. They have realised that Milosevic, who was elected president of Serbia in 1989, indoctrinated the Serbs into belligerent nationalism. My Croatian friends say that the

Muslim majority population in neighbouring Albania used to fleece and torture persons of Serb origin. After the fall of the communist government in Albania, Milosevic convinced the Serbs that this was a supreme opportunity to climinate non-Serbs from Kosovo and to declare it an ethnically cleansed Serb region. The Serbs failed to grasp Milosevic's extreme political ambitions and admitted him as their unchallenged champion to unleash a cycle of slaughter, arson, and loot. This inhuman racist violence is comparable only with Adolf Hitler's monstrous Holocaust. In the 1990 elections, the anti-imperialists emerged victorious in Slovenia, Croatia, Bosnia-Herzegovina, and Macedonia. Slovenia and Croatia declared themselves liberated. Milosevic straightaway sent in the army to crush the rebellion, resulting in unprecedented bloodshed and reducing around two million folks into hapless refugees.

Kresho Kernitz never gets weary of slamming the feeble and inconsistent policies of the UN in this period. I recall the refugees of 1947 in my nation—they had ransacked the bazaars of Delhi for food and protection from the cold. It is pointless to expect morality in a famished, banished crowd. Finally, the United Nations induced international treaties to subdue Milosevic's army, but it was a classic case of too little, too late. In these four long years, Milosevic had ordered his soldiers to engage in racial extermination for the formation of Greater Serbia. His policies were genocidal, merciless, and executed by the militia as well as common Serb citizens. Anyone trying to defy the orders of the Serb soldiers had to suffer inhumanly. America also played a conspiratorial role in pushing Yugoslavia into the civil war. The economic sanctions imposed by the USA and the NATO bombardment turned the life of the Serbs into hell. It was tragic, considering that these unsuspecting men and women had no time to spare from their profession and agriculture and that many of them had marriage relations with the Bosnians and the Croatians. David Hauberstam, in his book, *War in a Time of Peace*, has analysed the self-contradictions in American policies and branded America a power that perpetrates democratic and human right infringement perpetually on the pretext of establishing egalitarian regimes.

America unravels before me layer by layer. Many American feminists have collected and analysed the statistics on sexual violence against the Bosnian women. The statistics disturb me for two reasons. First, the Bosnian government pegs the rape cases at 50,000 (in reality it was much more), while the American NGOs claim a figure of 20,000. In their opinion, sexual savagery and rapes always follow a war. Another notion is that when the Bosnian and Croatian soldiers moved away to the frontline, the women left behind offered themselves to Serb soldiers, driven by desire and passion. The feminists instituted several such narratives in their reports submitted to the UN. Enloe, Otto, and Vance hypothesise that these women should stop thinking about sexual abuse and rape and move on to lead normal lives as their trysts during the war were mostly voluntary. Obviously, many of them must have dropped the idea of revealing their stories after such reports were published. Jesmia Husnawovic, a researcher on Bosnian and Herzegovinian women, exhorted them to ignore their hurts, swap grief for happiness and joy, and walk into the politics of hope through imagination and creativity, like warriors of political liberty.

***

Countless stories are scattered in the wind—stories of abuse, brutality, and torture—reinstating the idea that control over the woman's body is part and parcel of war strategy. It has three avowed objectives—first, to spread fear; second, forced dislocation; third, rewarding aggressors by letting them rape women. In developing countries, the issue of sexual violence against women, displacement, and insecurity can be analysed from the perspective of gender perceptions, sexuality, and collective identity. The tragedies of war produce topics for seminars and workshops, a lot of money is spent at the national and international levels on the collection of data and their analysis concerning the war, and we learn about the places where mass murders and other barbaric acts took place, spots like Kigali and Snebenika become tourist attractions. Those who are hungry to know about the dark chapters of human history find war spots quite useful. Research scholars conduct research on wars; both the scholars and experts visit the places and write exhaustive but indecipherable reports. Such incidents are used as raw material for arts and literature and by sociologists.

Time flies. It seems that these vigorous, beautiful-looking middle-aged women must have got over their humiliation and joined the mainstream because life eventually overwhelms all tragedies. However, the perception can be countered merely by one example—a Rogatia family from East Bosnia. All the women in their Bosnian home were raped by Serb soldiers—the grandmother, four daughters-in-law, and five granddaughters. A troop raided this extended, prosperous clan and set the men and children on fire. Their single crime was that they were Bosnian Muslims. Only the middle daughter-in-law has survived with a granddaughter. She has agreed to describe everything in detail, along with dates, but her nineteen-year-old daughter-in-law is averse.

***

Gradually, redemption will ebb,
Love one might seek but not need.
Wilt away will the anxiety to find, and the pain of losing,
Anger will not be alone, it will find mates.
An endless contest will ensue in which men
Will not fight for defeats
But to attest themselves.
And then will emerge cruelty.
First, it will settle in the heart but not appear on the face
And then it will happen in the interpretations of religious texts
Then in history and then in the prophecies;
It will turn into a creed,
The cry will go unheard

The second death will hold the tears spilt from the first death.
The neighbour will not offer solace but will whip out weapons
Then will settle down cruelty but it will not hurt our soul
And then it will appear on the face too
But will not be a marked emotion.
All faces will be alike
All of them shall kill and torment
And all shall be haughty
It will become a culture
And no one will resist it.
There will be efforts to make it look more sophisticated
With deeper roots in history
And it will rise as diffidence in future history
And soak away all our empathy
All our romance.
It is quite possible that it has already happened
But we won't know it has, for a long time.

—Kumar Ambuj

While talking with Ziba I recall this poem fervidly, titled *Cruelty*. Ziba remembers the gymnasium of her childhood school with a visible shudder. More than a hundred women were confined there with their suckling infants. Between fifteen and thirty-five—their most fertile age—the women were kept captive under ominous shadows of threats, intimidated by gun and grenade. And then commenced the vicious sport that put even cruelty to shame. Ziba reveals that the pregnant women were segregated; one group was of women with kids and another included girls that could be impregnated. Ziba's house was in East Bosnia. Her children were taken away from her when she entered the gaol. Women with kids were put to chores like cleaning floors, cooking, and fetching water. The children were kept under strict vigil because they knew the women would never desert their kids. Everything was carried out in the most organised manner in these rape camps. Fine-looking, tender-aged girls were fed on meat and bread and kept apart. Everybody except the girls themselves knew their fate.

One day, Ziba was ordered to remove her clothes. When she refused, they threatened to cut her throat. She was gang-raped continuously for twenty days. Most of the women that were already pregnant before they came here were killed. Stress, hunger, and beatings drove many of the women sick. Their foetuses were aborted and then they were abused remorselessly until they were impregnated by the Serb soldiers. The soldiers celebrated whenever a woman became pregnant. They claimed that their objective would not be achieved until all Muslim women of eastern and western Bosnia were filled with their virtuous semen. Sinad Sarik, who had managed to run away from a rape camp, described the condition of the women who were forced to bear children. The rest, driven into prostitution by the Serbs, vanished for years. Several years later a journalist traced them in Jablenica at Mostar by River Neretva. They knew their rapists. However, there was no atonement for them because they could not approach a tribunal or court of justice.

Seventy-one such unfortunate women were mowed down by machine guns in the neighbouring villages. The police were silent witnesses, no action was ever taken. These harmless, innocent, homely peasant women never beheld their children again. The only survivor noted down the details in her diary. When things returned to normal, some of them told reporters what they had undergone. They all accused Serb soldiers who called themselves White Eagles.

The nightmarish vision of inhuman killing and abuse congealed in the eyes of kids—hardly four or five years old—forever. Hassan from Kalinovic, barely four then, was an eyewitness to his mother's agony, but whenever he appeared in the court, he would begin to tremble and stutter. His evidence was considered unreliable. The Geko region from where Hasan comes has a 37 per cent Muslim population. They played a vital role in the economic and financial development of the region and emerged as a prosperous trader middle class in Bosnia. The Muslims who survived have endless, indescribable tales of torture to narrate. One says, 'We have watched the massacre of our people, we have seen naked women driven to drowning in the rivers, we have seen a Serb spitting on a mad, howling woman, clasping her dead infant to her bosom. What could be worse? We never thought we would live again to see the light of the day'. Terrified of the report that old men had been butchered, thousands of men and women from the villages of Basici, Drigovici, and Bahori escaped to the highland forests of Zelengora. Hundreds of children were separated from their families, wives lost husbands, mothers lost their kids. The men who went to the police were sent to Kosovo and Pristina and then to Skopje, the capital of Macedonia. The local officials of Skopje freed and shipped them to Muslim majority regions in Bulgaria, Romania, and Hungary.

An International Red Cross report states that a group of 200 Muslim women was rescued from the forest where they were hiding in graves. Many of them tried to escape without success. Sauda is one of the 209 girls who were caught while attempting to flee from the Serbs. She has written, 'There were twenty-four elderly people in our group. They were caught and dispatched to Olog. They were never seen again. The rest, numbering 185, were pushed onto open trucks in the pouring rain. We were transported to the camps and locked inside warehouses and toilets like animals. They used to take us to the gym. At first, their treatment was not really bad. We were ordered to carry water and cook. There was enough food; there were even friendly talks sometimes between the Serb guards and the prisoners. But shortly, the sentries were replaced by new ones. The new guards harried us with obscenities. One morning, a woman with long, brown tresses arrived and announced that she had been sent by the White Eagles. She asked us to remove the clothes of the children to verify if they had been circumcised. A new spell of continual rapes started. After the first night, Serb soldiers singled out teenagers and young girls and hustled them out. The girls were blubbering but none of the senior women had the nerve to help the wailing, bawling lambs. What could they do after all? It was everyone for herself. They dared not even sniffle. The girls were dragged one by one into the toilets by the gym that echoed with their pitiful cries. The birds caught in these forsaken valleys viewed the evil with horror. What is bigger—life or agony? Life, surely, since they remained alive despite the inhuman torture. The next morning, when the soldiers trooped in again, they mockingly called the girls by their names. The night had familiarised them with their victims. As soon as they started shoving a woman towards the toilets, her children would start screaming. The soldiers had suspicions that two of the women were merely pretending to be pregnant. They were forced to undergo a medical examination. However, after that, they did not endure rapes but were beaten frequently.

***

Dear Suman,

You have complained that I don't call you. Frankly, I don't feel like it. The stories of these women are so disturbing that I have begun to neglect everything. I often visit the market to buy provisions, cornflakes, and bread, but to tell you the truth, I am not up to it. The toothpaste that Ukki had requested for sparkling teeth, I have bought and packed it. I am also trying to learn Croatian. Still, it will be a lie if I say that I am happy. I am just pulling on. Sometimes loneliness appears lethal, as if you are trudging a lingering, interminable road. Do you remember? You had said once that life is not merely idyllic gazing at trees, clouds, and rains. Now I get it, how the study of chemistry has made you so hardnosed. The subjects we study do influence us. Habermas calls subjects like history, literature, philosophy, and sociology liberating disciplines in his work *Knowledge and Human Interest.* In today's world, teaching hotel management, business management, accounts, and information technology is considered reputable and more remunerative. In the neo-globalised liberal capitalism, the study of literature, history, and sociology, instead of fashion technology, appears pointless. Gradually, these disciplines are being pushed aside. We think and talk of the emancipation of the human being and his inner self yet these subjects are turning irrelevant. In several universities, the departments of languages, literature, and philosophy are languishing. The objective of knowledge is not only commerce and instant technological attainments. It should impart to us genuine values to create a better world. We must approach Theodor Adorno, Marx Weber, Erick Fromm, Walter Benjamin, and Herbert Marcuse for a veritable perception of modernity and industrial development because only they can offer us a genuine political analysis of cultural industrialisation, inform us on the different stages of development in a man's personality, and confirm that science cannot empathise if it is divested of conscience.

Rest is fine. I have gathered more information on Serbia and Bosnia. The soldiers that fought against the Turks during the Second World War were called Chetniks.

The members of the Serbian nationalist group too called themselves Chetnik. They believed that only when Muslim women started giving birth to small Chetniks would the objective of racial purity be achieved. Many of the women were sold in the Foka brothel because the Chetniks reaped sizable profits from these activities. Amna, 16; Suvada, 20; Amela, 17; and Miri, 16, were four such sisters—there was no trace of them for years after the war. Amela's mother, who herself was a victim of sexual violence, received a letter from her daughter after three years with the message that nobody should worry about her; that she had adopted a Serbian name and that her things should be sent to Foka.

The tales of horror in Kelinovic are endless. At this moment, as I am noting it down, I realise how one's heart can turn into stone. What must these school-going girls have felt when sick of daily rapes and abuse they accepted the profession of prostitution? Life is a blazing furnace for them. Do they remember their school, their home, their games and sports, parents—how they dreamt of the future? They must have cherished innumerable reveries, must have had friends, boyfriends; must have suffered the pain of thousands of unfulfilled promises. And then they would have put on a fake smile, learning the art of soliciting at an age they should have been in tender romantic trysts, learning the fortitude of keeping awake whole nights in their callow years, learning the art of amassing wealth at an age when they should have been playing chaste childhood games. Nalini Jamila has mentioned in her autobiography that for a woman, nothing can be worse than being called a whore. In India, it is still considered the most infernal profession. They have been given different names in ancient Indian literature—*rupajiva*, *panya-stree*, *ganika*, *nagarvadhu*, *lokangana*, *nartaki*, etc. A prostitute is defined as a woman who earns her livelihood in the open market. *Ganika* is the one who calculates what she earns—*ganayati iti ganika*. *Rupajiva* sells her beauty. *Panya-stree*—a woman bought with money. In *Arthashastra*, Kautilya has mentioned the employment of *ganika*s to train men from the royal family in manners, literature, and music. These women do not object to being called *veshya* and consider themselves professional workers. Many of them assist their families with their earnings. Don't worry about me. Many a time I don't feel like writing letters or talking. I have not called anyone in Delhi for a long time. Sometimes the visit to the edge detaches us from the centre. The weather must be good in Delhi. You are such a great scientist, but tell me, have you faced gender discrimination ever in PUSA or not? You are close to my heart so I needn't hide my tears from you, I can tell you. Take care.

Rest awhile.

Yours,

Garima.

***

It is the month of Shravan. The trees in the cvjetni-cesta are teeming with blossoms and leaves, and people who never came out on the streets are emerging. Still, it is a gale outside and you need at least a windcheater. I notice the signboard of a salon on the ground floor of the building across ours, Frijreski Salon. I wonder why I never paid attention to it earlier. Customers are welcomed warmly in the hairdresser salon. The employees are young girls and boys—from eighteen to twenty-five. It is a unisex facility. Those desiring privacy can hire cabins. They probably have to pay extra. A horse-faced, skinny girl whose hair is dyed in myriad tints, asks me, '*Sto jelis?*' Do I need hair grooming? She is wearing an apron with an assortment of scissors, stylers, curlers, clips, combs, and hair brushes in its innumerable pockets. She begins to work on me. Across the translucent curtain on the left, I can see two girls performing a cross-massage in low light. Several youths from Thailand and Indonesia are considered experts in cross-massage. They earn substantially—many rich customers enjoy corporeal fulfilment. The new Croatian generation is fashionable and knows how to boost their earnings through diverse techniques of cross-massaging. In India, there are many taboos attached to cross-massage; here there is none. The head and body massage for the treatment of insomnia, migraine, and other mental ailments by the opposite gender is a part of it. Research has proved that it is useful in sports injuries. Lavender oil reduces swellings and hides the years and the wrinkles; menstrual problems and cancer also are treated through massages. Across Europe, Kundalini massage and Tantra massage are costly rubdowns imported from oriental nations—it is another form of cross-bodywork. Dushka has told me that massage from the lowest vertebrate of the spine to the lower part of the neck with the essence of flowers and a mixture of oils rekindles lost sensations.

The salon girl looks at the cabin and says, '*Ya mogu wam dati massaga pre vice*' (I can give a massage before more). I reply, '*Trebam oasisaam*' (I simply need a haircut). The girl is not disheartened, she makes an offer, '*Mogu vam ponuditi veliki popust na masažu*' (I can offer you a big discount on the massage). My stern demeanour makes her focus on my haircut. She plasters avocado and ripe papaya pulp on my face. I grin, looking at myself in the mirror, and recall Dragitsa. She has written in her will that a beautician should have her face made up when she dies and that her hearse should be a black Rolls Royce. Obviously, she wants to leave a lasting, favourable impression on her friends and relatives even in death.

The human heart is a funny thing; its tenacity for life even in the worst of situations is amazing. The neighbours have informed me that the owners of the hairdressing salon—all of them women—stay in Vokowar (Eastern Croatia)—Rujia Barbarik, 63; Snezana Maljek, 47; and Maria Sliskovic, 50. It has several outlets. These women were abused sexually during the attacks by the Serbian soldiers in Vukowar in November 1991. The Croatian government has been trying to enact a bill to assist such victims. As I revise the notes in my journal on May 2015, the Croatian minister Fred Matic has announced the provision for paying 100,000 kunas to every sexually abused woman located anywhere in the world, along with a stipend of 2,500 kunas a month, free medical treatment, and legal counselling. It is an initiative to put salve on twenty-year-old injuries. Dushka tells me on Skype that very few women will be willing to accept the compensation. Many women buried their agony and did not even lodge a complaint. Their children are grown up. If they come ahead, their wounds would fester again. To announce their disgrace publicly is unimaginable. What is worse, is the annual visit to the government hospital to acquire the certificate that they really suffered the abuses years ago. The victims hold different opinions on the compensation. One says, 'Better late than never. Justice is not merely a word, it should translate into action. This law will certainly improve my life financially but what is more important is that it has made me feel once more that I am a human being'. Another declares, 'No amount of compensation can make up for what I have suffered; I want nothing but justice'.

Verika Martirnovic's family scattered after the violence and she was left alone to fend for herself. Today, at the age of fifty-five, she has involved several other women in her fashion business. She says, 'Your soul, your mind, heart, the body, are stigmatised after rape—you can treat the physical wounds but what about the mental ones? Who would like to taste a cur's leftovers?' The new act has come as a symbolic relief to Croatian women; however, one must go through a protracted legal process to establish that she was abused. This clause dissuades many women. Mladen Lonkar analyses the psychological aspect as she lights one cigarette after another, 'When the law favours the exploited, they find associates to share their suffering and finally gather the courage to come out in the open'. Maria Slikovic runs an NGO called 'Women in the Homeland'—she has been working for rape victims of the war since 2000. Stout and hard-working, Maria has seen the world. She does not hesitate in speaking about the Croatian women. The new law has helped these women articulate their agony. She takes me to Hervatinek's husband who is around sixty. He visits the NGO regularly to keep his wife mentally healthy. He has been witnessing her agony for the last twenty years. 'She asks me to leave her. Rape has changed my sunny, sociable mate harshly. We have seen the worst of days. It is not unusual to see a marriage being destroyed under such circumstances but nobody who has not witnessed or not been a victim of the abuses can ever understand it. My wife tried to kill herself and me several times. The Serbs wrecked her mentally and physically. She used to weep whole nights but I did not even once think of deserting her. I can't narrate some of the things she did. Even to this day, she is like a small girl in need of extensive care.' What Maria told me after the gentleman departed shook me to the core. I was stunned to hear that she was assaulted together by twenty Serbs.

An important issue on the nine-point agenda of the Voice of the Women's Liberation Front was the sharing of the experiences of the abused women among themselves so that they might recognise, understand, and express the attitudes outside and inside the home. Also, it should be publicised widely. In principle it sounds good, but in real life, it is quite different. Guldane, Dora, and Smokey prefer to remain silent on the subject. Guldane is from Turkey but she is pretty familiar with the cultural and social manners of the Bosnian Muslims. Guldane and I share our joys and sorrows, the happening in our countries, and our rites and rituals. She often comes down to my flat to enjoy Hindi songs. I also await these visits eagerly because she is sentimental like me. She wants to wear an Indian *lehenga* in her marriage. She can cook a couple of Turkish dishes and relishes my cheese *parathas*. She does not know much about the war victims of Croatia, Serbia, and Bosnia, but she can speak English and Turkish fluently. She also wants Turkey to join the European Union. I suspect now and then that she does not like my collecting reports of the war victims. We love shopping together.

She tells me that she is sick of her treatment at the Turkish embassy in Zagreb. They keep calling her to demonstrate their superiority and offer needless advice concerning her stay here. It does not matter what rank a woman holds, she is constantly made aware of the fact that she is an underling. It is an unremitting grind for Guldane. Thank god, my life is comparatively undisturbed; our embassy officials treat me in a friendly manner. They respect my space. I too keep my distance, seeing them only on special occasions or at functions. Women have to devise a strategy to maintain their dignity or else society would wolf them down. There is this Mr Bhatia, middle-aged, retiring in September; he has missed promotion to the post of the First Secretary. He has been acting weirdly these six months before his imminent retirement; perhaps he is not mentally prepared to be a pensioner yet. It has unhinged him slightly—he often makes himself an object of laughter. Why does the probability of superannuation usually disturb people? It is pretty common in India. Retiring people in our nation generally have no plans for the future and the eventual shift of the relationships within the family upsets them. Our women accept it more easily as they occupy themselves in the family or take up the hobbies left behind. On the other hand, men start feeling lonely because they are hounded by the fear of being dislocated from the position of the master in the family, and the lack of an alternative skill turns them restive. Bhatiaji has spent most of his life abroad. He speaks English with a Punjabi accent and always compares India to hell. The royal dinners, wine binges, and gifts from the Indian embassies in different countries are his surviving capital, he eventually has to bid goodbye to the embassy at Zagreb for his native 'Jullundher'.

***

The war in this part of Eastern Europe forced a large number of women into prostitution. I discovered it accidentally when one of my students, Miri Anna, got into a heated discussion over the issue of her college fees. She argued that Zagreb University charged a hefty fee and several students like her had to work themselves to death during the vacations to arrange it. Her native place is Arizona Market. In Bosnia, Arizona Market is spread over thirty-five acres; it was settled and publicised internationally as a centre to improve relations between Serbs, Croatians, and

Bosnians after the war. Anna's description was a shocking one. During the war, it was a market for consumer goods and sundry international wares as well as merchandise from the villages. However, a different face of the market surfaced when the war got over in December 1995. The four-year conflict had destroyed the Bosnian economy. One can imagine the enormity of the plunge by the fact that while the average annual income of the common man was 2,400 dollars before Sarajevo fell, by 1995, it had plummeted to 500 dollars. By the time the war finished, almost 80 per cent of the Bosnian population had lost their jobs. Those who retained them were in the police, schools, and municipal departments because they had strong connections in the government or had used their political affiliations. A few, mostly women, were employed in international organisations. These establishments in post-war Bosnia-Herzegovina required women with degrees in English and Sociology, women who could work with total commitment at ludicrously low wages. Nobody had an idea about those who never had any opportunities. What work did they take up? Was it this most odious, wicked, and immoral profession? What fate did these little educated and badly needy women in hundreds suffer?

I am overwhelmed. In India, the women joining this profession are disdained by society in the light of the day. Policemen posted in red light areas are delighted as if they have hit the jackpot, whether it is Sonagachhi in Kolkata, Chaturbhuj Sthan in Muzaffarpur, Dalmandi in Benaras, Kamathipura in Mumbai, Mirganj in Allahabad, Budhwar Paith in Pune, or Garstin Bastion Road in Delhi. Does anyone really bother about these women who peddle their bodies? Do they remain human beings anymore? No, they are reduced into shrewd market cargo by learning how to deal with the extortionists, pimps, and law-keepers, jotting down the sums they pay each one as if they were predestined for this career. Do they ever dream of a home or family? After the last customer is done with, they too must yearn for an intimate, reassuring smell, someone who caresses the hollow rings around their eyes fondly, senses the disquiet clutching their soul, and whispers softly that it is the body that is sullied, not the heart. It is a means of livelihood, don't fight the world for its sake, there is good also around us. Listen to the melody of the dawn after the exhausting night and fill your lungs with the scent of the clouds to douse the fetor. Let bygones be bygones, take up a respectable profession. One can always begin life anew. Ironically, if a woman adopts the occupation on a personal footing in India, it is not a breach of law, but brothels are deemed illegal. In Mumbai alone, there are more than 100,000 sex workers. They are merely female bodies that are not supposed to have the luxury of emotions. The police, the administration, the pimps, and this hypocritical world are a weird realm—there is no room for civil language. It cannot afford the extravagance of conscience in the thick of insults, snatchings, hormone and drug injections, cheap attar, and tacky silk dresses.

***

Why I have engaged in this task of uncovering the economic,

social, and legal position of the sex workers in distant Europe is beyond me. Possibly, wars impact children and women the most. I intend to visit Arizona Market but I have hit a dead end. Miri is unwilling to take me there. Maybe she works as a sex worker during vacations. Her mom also is there.

***

We remember places visited in the past because they evoke memory and occasionally, a specific image is fixed in the psyche. One should go to an alien land only if someone awaits him or her there eagerly. On the contrary, I very well realise that nobody other than my bookshelves wait for me at home. One does not return home simply because one must, but because somebody is sleeping there fitfully, expecting her by his side. A home offers more than comfort and safety; it also attests that you exist, over and over again. People that lose their homes and have no possibility of returning, their life turns into a thoroughfare that can be trampled at will.

Guldane Kalin has planned a trip to Poyetno this week. Dora's native village, Poyetno, is some 35 kilometres from Zagreb. She left three days ago. Guldane and I are travelling together—we will board the train at the main station of Zagreb, Glavni Kolodvor. The ticket costs fifty kunas to and fro. The coach resembles those of the Shatabdi Express in India. The curtains are old, the gloss has faded. The seats too are timeworn but are wide and clean; the ticket examiner appears in a spotless uniform and cap. The commuters are quiet; it is not noisy as on Indian trains. The train leaves unhurriedly, on time. Gul and I strike up a conversation. Outside the window, there is a boundless expanse of the bright, azure sky. The train climbs an incline slowly, it stops at a couple of stations for a minute or two; a few passengers get on. The platform is deserted, the stone benches are desolate, there are tall pine trees with pointy leaves. The guard in a black uniform and white cap swings the green flag at the tall, brown, wooden doors of the stark white building of the station. The train moves and the vendor's shout in India surfaces in my memory—'tea, hot tea!' It is different here.

Guldane is dozing; I recall the Bolpur station in India. The track has recently converted from metre to broad gauge and I am not yet comfortable walking across to the other platform via the overhead bridge. There are hawkers selling *jhalmuri*, *shasha* (cucumber), *shingara* (*samosa*), *dim* (egg), *sonpapdi*, *sitabhog*—the station is filled with clamour. There are as many vendors as passengers. If you have a deep pocket and powerful digestion, food like *seddha dim* (boiled egg) and fine *khoya*-filled *sitabhog* of Bardhaman district beckons you with open arms. '*Kato kore* (how much)?' '*Panch taka, dash taka*' (five rupees, ten rupees)—eat to your heart's fill! The journey will finish but the array of snacks stretches endlessly. Lo, the *jhalmuri* seller is here! The shrewd *muri* seller recognises the daily commuters. He calls you *Didi* if you are a lady, and *Dada* if you are a man, and whip-mixes parched rice, slices of boiled potato, finely chopped onion, green chillies, lemon, and *chat masala* in the most meticulous proportions in a tin can with its upper half removed, tempting the palate with the sharp tang of the sprinkled mustard oil, topped up with a white, vigorous sliver of coconut poised like the second day's moon. He serves *jhalmuri* in half-snipped paper bags, rattling his brass spoon all the while—you promptly whisk out a ten rupee note for the delicacy. A *samosa wallah* arranges rows of crispy *samosas* in his basket and just then, the public address system crackles the arrival of the Kanchanjungha Express. The *samosa wallah* is in a tearing hurry—he must cross the tracks—the signal has already turned green. He lowers the basket onto the tracks, jumps down, and picks it up again. He sprints across the tracks but finds it difficult to heave the basket onto the other platform. Passengers pull him up; the basket also is on the platform now but many of the *samosas* have fallen on the track. He leaps down and puts the *samosas* on the platform lightning quick. The train engine is racing towards him. The platform shudders from the thunder of the approaching behemoth, people call out desperately—he springs. He is back on the platform, safe with all his *samosas* on the platform floor! The train has arrived, the *coolies* (porters) dash to the sleeper and AC (air conditioned) compartments, while the *samosa wallah* cleans the *samosas* with his Kolkata cotton towel with its red, checkered pattern. The crusty, fresh *samosas* are displayed immaculately once again and he is back in business with his ringing call, '*Shinghara khaben*!' (Have *samosas*!)

The train is speeding towards Poyetno. Guldane is morose remembering her Australian lover—she prefers silence. A Croatian woman on the single seat after two rows on the left is carrying a large vanity bag. She glances around and opens the flap—there is a whole beauty salon inside! The old woman who boarded the train at Zagreb station has magically transformed into a young, beautiful lass in fifteen minutes. False eyelashes and the wig are a sorcerer's wand, she is painting her nails with extreme concentration. She pouts and looks at her reflection in the mirror and assured, slips on her pencil heel sandals. Greasepaint has boosted her self-confidence. She stands at the gate to get off self-importantly. Looking at this woman, who can imagine that the Croatians witnessed war and skirmishes for five odd years and suffered inhuman tortures and pains? In such a background, her heavy makeup does not seem out of place, rather, it increases my respect for the dignified disposition of this resilient community. Women adapt themselves to the changing times quickly.

Poyetno station is in sight. I touch Guldane's hand lightly. We get up. Dora is waiting at the platform.

***

I wonder about the fate of the hundreds and thousands of women who suffered physical abuse and financial hardships. Did they lose their will to live or did they choose an alternative road? Government initiatives are not sufficient to provide a livelihood to all the victims of the conflict zones. I have read somewhere that Arizona Market harbours a spider web of illicit businesses. Serbs, Croatians, Romanians, Bulgarians—all sorts of nationalities are involved in the shady deals. Alexandra Stiglmayer has given the details in her book *Mass Rape: The*

War against Women in Bosnia-Herzegovina, about how in post-war Bosnia, Arizona Market has prospered as a centre for international woman trafficking. There are girls of all ages. Hapless women who fell victim to trafficking. Peace soldiers were deployed here by the UN, to develop the market into a showcase settlement where citizens of these countries might be rehabilitated after the war. The international committee was in favour of free and fair elections for the reconstruction of Bosnia to usher in a stable democracy, but it did not happen because the human rights organisations failed to take lead.

The committee had proposed to include women in the negotiation process too because the people working in the gender field believed that women performed better in NGOs. Astonishingly, the international organisations treated Bosnian women merely as statistics to analyse the conditions in post-war Bosnia. They might have concealed their war trauma and torture under the armour of smiles to refurbish their country, but their colleagues and the organisations saw them only as rape case studies. Their narratives of torture were to be studied as academic reports all over the world. After the war, the women disregarded their grief to confer on models of development yet they were deliberately kept out of the policy-making process. They were degraded into sheer sites of exploitation. On the other hand, in Arizona Market, prostitution and slavery emerged as a rapidly growing commercial segment, since they provided buyers and sellers on an international level. A large number of foreign soldiers and civil servants deployed here swapped roles to turn buyers.

***

I have resolved that until I get permission to visit Bosnia again, I will keep collecting information on Arizona Market and Kosovo. Bars and eateries mushroomed in this district after the war, generating large-scale employment for local and foreign girls. A meeting of the Committee on Equal Opportunities for Women and Men was held in The Hague on 14 and 15 November 2002. The critical discussion in the session resulted in vital resolutions, including delivering legal assistance to sex workers, protection at the workplace, and health safeguards. The Council of the European Parliamentary Assembly also studied the causes and effects of sex trafficking and suggested measures to check it. The issue of human trafficking is also linked with displacement. Human trafficking is illegal, as well as the most depraved line of work, but the bitter reality is that it is firmly institutionalised. Usually, corruption makes it flourish during spells of displacement. Displaced people can be manipulated easily without any fear of reprisal. It is a mockery of human rights. In fact, no country can tackle this problem singlehanded because it involves people, police, and the power centres of multiple nations. Human and drug trafficking are interlinked, although the risk factor is higher in drug trafficking. Child and woman trafficking require comparatively less investment but they also take longer.

Illiteracy, hunger, and unemployment affect women more strongly than men. It becomes customarily the woman's duty to take care of the home and kids and to feed them, especially after the loss of men in a war. It is not always possible to provide every woman with her preferred job. The number of unemployed women in most of Europe is considerably high; several European countries have shut their borders to displaced people. Uprooted people fall easily into the trap of agents to manage their illegal entry into countries with stringent migration laws. A few modifications were introduced in 1990 when economic liberalisation compelled many nations to reconsider their migration policies. The inability of the displaced to fight their cases in court, widespread poverty, and the lack of sufficient legal information has spiked human trafficking in the last twenty years, especially of women and sex workers. There was a huge surge in sex trafficking after the fall of the Berlin Wall because the borders of Eastern Europe had opened. It was abetted by the deteriorating economic conditions in the eastern socialist blocs, resulting in a greater number of women being pushed into the net of sex trafficking. Prior to this, women were brought in from Asian countries. Later on, they were lured from Eastern European countries to France and Italy during the economic depression, with prospects of jobs as domestic help, or work in hotels and restaurants. They were tempted and trapped with promises of better earnings. These women were taken to Hungary or Romania clandestinely; they had no legal documents. The allure of good jobs and the assurance of illegal but safe entry into another country were used as bait. Once they fell into the trap, their passports were taken away on the pretext of obtaining visas. They were transported to Serbia through Hungary and pushed into a blind tunnel, escaping which was almost impossible. Join prostitution or submit eventually through repeated rapes and beatings—there was no getaway. Many of the women capitulated when they witnessed the torture of others. Sometimes they were raped repetitively before being handed over to some bar or café owner. They kept mute out of fear. The owners forced them into submission through sexual debasement, thrashing, and physical abuse. The new 'Masters' trafficked them to other countries illegally in small trucks and cars, through back country roads and rivers on dark nights, before another batch arrived. Sex trafficking transpired on a large scale in disturbed border areas. It is still a lucrative business in post-war Europe and several other countries, but it was astonishingly high during the periods of war and displacement. Every woman I have met has a personal story, still, they are all interconnected. I remember the protest of hundreds of naked women in Manipur against the brutal rape and murder of Manorama in July 2004. Do human sensibilities survive in a woman after her rape?

Look at us,
We are billowing streamers of naked flesh
See, in the middle of the square we stand with our breasts bared;
The breasts in the middle of which
You wanted to plant the tricolour.
See our naked thighs in the open,
These are the thighs
On which you have branded the anthem of your manhood.
We have walked out in the streets naked
Like the frustrated, tortured land of Manipur

Wriggling under boots.
Tell your nation to stare at us
Command your state to rape us,
Advise your civilisation to
Crush our heads and chuck them in the forest.
Order your militia to
Chop off our little fingers
And decorate them like medals on their uniforms.
We have walked out naked on the streets
Like our naked questions.
We have walked out on the roads
Like stark lightning in the sky;
Without a string on our stripped bodies
We are billowing streamers of naked flesh.

—Anshu Malviya

A girl called Celia, petite and charming, is a sex worker here. She had a different name but a Chinese customer once called her 'silly' and the name stuck. She was born in the slums but at the young age of seven she was shipped to drudge as a maidservant. By the age of eleven, she had grown accustomed to rape by her master. At the age of fifteen, the elderly master proposed marriage to her but she refused. She tells me, 'A neighbour approached me and I set off with the starry dream of a new, shining world. I was smuggled into the UK with five other women'. She was lured by the prospect of a janitor's job but the reality was different. Her first master told him that she would have to slog as a sex worker to pay for the passage to the UK, the travel expenses, and food. 'It was a rigorous two-year sentence—I was hauled to a string of customers. Once, a customer called Carlos paid me sixty pounds in one go. I saw a chance and escaped, running madly, blindly to the police station, but my travails were not yet over. I ached to return to my family, to insist my mother rub me clean with a towel as she used to do when I was a child, to seek haven in her lap, away from the evil eyes. I'll do whatever you tell me, Mumma, please save me this once!'

'What happened next?' I ask her.

There is a deathly dreariness in her brown, vacant eyes, 'The police informed me that my visa had expired—I had not the slightest idea. They debated among themselves, was my arrival in the country lawful or illegal? They were least bothered about what I had suffered; their only concern was my visa. I was confined in a detention centre, it was worse than prison. There were all sorts—beggars, thieves, drug addicts. They used to laugh at me—if I had broken away, why did I go to the police station? My depression built up, nobody was willing to listen to me. I tried to commit suicide but I was saved and they imposed a stricter vigil. I was not allowed to visit even the washroom alone. It was so sickening that I often thought that I was much better off as a sex worker. There were other women too—victims of trafficking—in the detention centre. The cops interrogated me to identify the traffickers who had smuggled me into the UK. They were more interested in catching the illegal immigrants living there without a valid visa. Finally, they sent me to Bosnia. I have been in Zagreb for many years and have developed contacts with several tourist agencies. I work as an escort now to help my family in Bosnia financially. This is the only profession I know'.

***

I have met a woman from Albania with a similar story. She was married off by her irresponsible father at the age of nineteen. Her husband left for Greece in search of a job. She received nothing but abuse and neglect at her in-laws. Eventually, she joined a beautician course where a man began to commiserate with her. He took her to the UK and pushed her into prostitution. There were two other Albanians with her. 'When I refused, I was whipped with leather belts. I was kept confined in a room; rape and beating were routine. I had to cater to at least five customers every day. It was futile to attempt escape because the traffickers knew my family and village well. One day, the door remained open accidentally and unable to check myself, I ran away barefoot. Fortunately, I met two women from Kosovo in the market. They lent me clothes and food. I did not approach the police because they would have dispatched me back to Albania.' I am recording this interview and therefore I don't interrupt her. She adds, 'I communicated my problems to an NGO but they were least interested. I was advised to put in an application for a women's shelter but it was rejected because I had been a sex worker and also because I had tried to run away. I was not considered trustworthy. I appealed in court, and narrated my story at every bureau, in the council office, home ministry—but nobody helped me. My life was like a burning asphalt road without a hint of shade. No ray of hope. I was two months pregnant when I ran away. I was asked to name the father in every hospital. No one pitied me; it was after a dreadful ordeal that I was accepted in the shelter home for a year on a court order. When I came out, I had no job and being on the brink of starvation, I decided to take up sex work again to muster two square meals for myself and my child. I am still a streetwalker with an uncertain future'. A twenty-first century European woman, yet she suffers the same abuses that one endured in the medieval ages. She has no expectations from society, the government, or the establishment. She is just a flesh vessel in which men expel their semen. Beyond this, she is an object of hate, spurned because of her vulnerability and terminal diseases. How is her condition different from the woman in a feudal, patriarchal community? A woman, often used as a honey trap, is an object for sexual satisfaction, to satiate one's appetite for carnal beauty during peacetime. She is a commodity, a thing, a body. Not a human being.

***

Many NGOs in Bosnia-Herzegovina are convinced that it is more important to rehabilitate these women rather than rescue them. For years, K. Katawic has been helping women who have managed to quit the profession. He says, 'Countless women are in sex work to keep their body and soul together, but when they walk out, they suffer abjectly from want of any other skill. They earn plenty here. No other occupation in the unorganised sector pays so well. Unsurprisingly, despite all efforts, they often re-join the profession'.

***

So many women with identical tales. Ethiopia's Elini was handed over to the traffickers by her own father, 'They arranged my passport and visa and told me I was supposed to work in a household in Berlin. The conditions were disgusting. The master of the house raped me, ravaged me, and even the mistress of the house lent a hand in the abuse. My salary was often withheld. Still, I was at least getting food every day. Soon after, they left for France and I was instructed to go back to my country. I was afraid I would be jailed like my father the moment I set foot in Ethiopia, so I fled in terror. Disoriented, I walked for miles and when I was exhausted, I plopped down on a bench in a public park. A man in the park handed me over to the police. The police put me in a women's hostel, then in a shelter home, and finally in a detention centre because I had no visa. When I came out, I was a mental wreck. I had no option. In the end, I turned back to my old profession. There was no support, no help, what choice did I have?'

Her question has disturbed me. They state the truth—reward, punishment, morality, and immorality do not matter for persons who sorely need a roof over their heads and food in their belly. Since most of us are blessed with a home without any effort, and since most of us have not suffered real difficulties, the poetry of our life flows on. We do not even notice how many other women on the same planet cannot afford a wall to even bang their heads on. They are forbidden to dream, they are forbidden the music of life, they are forbidden love. They are reduced to mere flesh, a body, an object they sell for a few pieces of silver. Nobody loves them, nobody fancies them, nobody wants them, they are but a commodity.

They cast off their sense of shame, their consciousness, and their dignity to knock on the shadowy hotel and guest-house doors. If a fellow craves a raunchy romp, at least they will take home some money to manage meals for a day, a week, a month. No one likes them, nobody tolerates them. They become escorts or call girls because they do not want to live like beggars. They recognise the price of their flesh, moulded by God—He, who produced the rich and also the poor. He sent them out to earth and forsook them—go, fend for yourself! Bop like a puppet, I will enjoy the *tamasha* from paradise and snicker. You will bow your head at my door, you will sing paeans of my compassion in churches, kneel on the prayer mat, and confess your imagined sins, sobbing ceaselessly. I will laugh at your emotions, warmth, affection, and generosity, observing your sell-off like a lifeless chunk of flesh.

There are innumerable women waiting fervently for the clouds of compassion, swallowing insults, pleading guilty, resolving to give up the past and live life afresh but the promises of succour are scarce—no benefactor ever shows up. Like someone scooping water from a river to quench their thirst and then putting it out of their mind. Rarely does anyone indulge them with genuine kindness; the majority regard them as objects. Angelina once told me, 'Miracles happen only in movies. We get customers of all ages, from teenagers to toothless old men. Teenagers make us uncomfortable because they are full of weird ideas. Mostly middle-aged men come to us for emotional support when they feel neglected by their wives and family. Usually rich, they narrate their teary tales of mistreatment in the family and leave after spending quality time with us.

They are our biggest chunk. They need someone to listen to them compassionately. To talk and gratify the physical urge, but they also waste a lot of our time. Elderly customers sometimes act funny in their attempt to prove themselves. Still, we don't react because we get money in return. Maybe he has bad breath, maybe he is teeming with diseases, still, if he can pay, we are willing. We can't refuse because it is bad for business. Nobody bothers about our sulks—we understand best the value of money. Pimps, cops, bartenders, everyone is greedy for dough. A couple of teenage customers do get emotionally involved but they lack real money. Customers with financial stability also have children and families to look after. They are boastful but our profession has trained us to size up the customers. Middle-aged men often make up stories of their wives' cruelty to win our hearts. They are in search of love as well as passion. Some of us are taken in yet their yearning for a dignified life and home does not die. You will find many such duped women falling mentally ill. Except for the rare hardnosed ones, there is hardly a sex worker who does not crave a real husband, a home, and kids. Some fortify themselves to lead a balanced professional life and save money. But by the time they reach middle age, they go silly and sick, some of them turn into junkies, some still wait for customers that never turn up. Frustration and depression hollow them from inside.'

I find it difficult to listen. I feel like getting up, holding their hands, and telling them that it is hell they are living in. Run away, bolt, take up any other work but not this. In fact, it is my traditional, moral Indian upbringing on the move. These women are accustomed to living and breathing this profession, they have also learnt to wait for the end. In the afternoons, some of them train in film songs and new dance styles. A couple of customers like singing and dancing; their own wives would never do it. 'Some customers demand to see the medical certificate, some are utterly reckless; however, they all are honourable citizens in daylight. Some are regulars. One of them even paid for my pension insurance', Marina smiles. Oscar Wilde has said that a life terminating in the middle is full since the future perishes with it. When did the lives of these women commence? When would it close? Will it ever begin or simply crumble? Without hope, without expectations, sometimes with pimps, sometimes with their own children sired by nameless fathers, sometimes plunging down the abyss of addiction, sometimes faking music and dance, sometimes trying to please, trying to ignore the cries and sobs of unborn children, masking the wrinkles on the face with greasepaint, lifting the bust with cheap push-up bras, using mouth fresheners, roving in the latest fragrances and miasmas, envious of the youthful whores, cursing their own febrile, writhing bodies under stinking quilts in damp, freezing rooms, absolutely miserable.

Licking fingers to count euros and dollars, painting their cracked nails, and scrubbing the body vehemently sometimes to wash away the filth accumulated in the soul with water, when will their life begin? When will it get over? They learn to disremember the past. They don't want to dredge up who pushed them into this inferno; they have forfeited poise in life, only the anticipation of the ensuing evening accompanied by moolah, liquor, merriment, and the amnesia of grief can fill them with some warmth.

There will be reckonings, auctions of the flesh, and contests shall be won on the strength of youth and artifice. For a few hours, they shall forget their pains and abuses in the headiness of intoxication and wondrously transform into queens and princesses; in the glittering strobes of the night among exciting smoke clouds, they would transmute into the most desirable virgin-whores!

***

The narratives reveal the post-war conditions of thousands of Bosnian and Serbian women. The American feminist Catherine MacMillan has pointed out the regressive role of the peace soldiers in Bosnia, mentioning that the presence of the UN here amplified women trafficking, brothels, massage parlours, peep shows, and the production of pornographic films. UN officials and soldiers were deployed in the region to foster goodwill and peace, but the move triggered an increase in the demand for sex workers and generated employment for uprooted women, pimps, and traffickers. In 1999, human rights organisations discovered brothels stuffed with local and exotic women like cattle. They had no passports and no IDs. Most of the women remained silent but a few came ahead to record their travails.

The subsequent report condemned their trading from one sex house to another, the poundings, and intimidation. The UN published a list of 260 such night clubs but the NGOs came up with a shocking figure of more than a thousand, scattered all over Bosnia, where sex trafficking was flourishing right under the nose of the police and the administration. Each of the clubs held hostage four to twenty-five women. A Human Right Watch report in May 2000 mentioned that the local and international police and peacekeeping forces contributed substantially to sex trafficking. More than 60 per cent of customers were foreigners, and a large mass came from the peacekeeping soldiers. The international share in the sex revenue was 72 per cent. Before the war, the economic condition of Serbia was better than that of several other East European countries, but later on, it converted into an interim centre for trafficking and transit. Most of the women from Ukraine, Russia, and Romania were introduced into the trade by way of Serbia. They spent their initial days as sex workers in Serbia, after which they were unloaded to other agents in Italy through Montenegro. The situation was not any better in Macedonia. Montenegro's geographical location made it a convenient centre for NATO soldiers; it was also the location where the Albanian mafia had entrenched itself. Trafficked women from Bulgaria, Ukraine, Mongolia, Romania, and Albania were sent to the Middle East and Western Europe via Greece. They were bought and sold regularly. One speculation is that they changed hands three to six times by the time they arrived in Kosovo.

***

The weather is frigid, windy, and wet. My heart cries when I ponder over the fate of these women. Their grief and groans have taken over my consciousness. Their only crime is that they possess a woman's form, and therefore, they are denied the dignity of a human being. The body is the major site of exploitation. If I preferred, I could return to India during the end semester vacations but the very thought of a day-and-a-half of air travel makes me jittery. I plan to meet Kathryn Bolkovec during the vacation. Mislav has told me only that she has worked in Sarajevo, the Bosnia capital, nothing more. There are plenty of NGOs overseeing post-war cases and rehabilitation of rape victims but they are unable to tell me much. Nobody discloses anything unless you know them personally. I should also get hold of Rees, who rehabilitates sex workers. Maybe I will manage it this month with the help of Rinato Pitak, who imports Asian and Indian goods and sells them here.

***

Day and night, sleeping or awake, these uprooted women haunt me. During the slack period, I went to a flower show in Zagreb. Masses of flowers, dazzling decorations—every flower flourished an invitation. Had Manjudi been here, she would have drowned me in a whole heap of information regarding the medicinal properties of the plants and their etymology. Sadly, none of them bears a fragrance. I chance upon several friends in the show, some are eager to view their first dusky Indian in an Indian dress, some gawk at me in astonishment, some look down upon me haughtily, while a few glance casually.

As I gaze at the flower pots, I grow emotional. I recall the *patabahar* and the golden *amaltas*; the brighter the sun, the more vivid they shone. I also recall Shyamali yelling, 'Tie your hair in a bun!' And when the coiffure was done, one man objected. 'Who told you to do this?' He had murmured softly, 'I long to unravel your curly tresses with my fingers, breathe the *nagchampa* perfume on you. Haven't heard of it? Silly girl! It grows riotously in the hill forest. Come to me, you will mingle with its incense; an unforgettable experience!' Who was this stranger, stretching out his hand? He did not ask me even once to stay back. We used to go on long walks together yet my curly hair remained tangled forever. Is it easy to unravel things? Nothing is ever resolved, neither our self nor our lives. Each of us has to walk our own road like puppets swinging to background music. An entire life is consumed in prancing to the tune. What survives is lesser wishes, myriad smells, and a haunting image—a hand waving forlornly in the window. How to recreate the bygone moments? There are no replays in life. When the rains are over, raindrops too forsake the coconut leaves.

Yesterday, it was squally and showery in Turkebana as I waited for the tram—my umbrella whipped off the moment I loosened my grip intentionally. A tall, academic sort of lad was looking at me—he smiled when our eyes met. I was embarrassed a bit. What must have he thought! He would not know that I never disrupt the getaway of people or moments. Not once did I spread my arms to declare to anyone, '*Ami jete debo na tomake*' (I would never let you go). And this was merely a paltry umbrella. The rain poured over me next to the blackstone statue of King Kreshomir with its squat legs. My hair streamed in the braiding, dishevelling wind. Trams headed to Vienisk came and left. I listened to the torrent pattering bountifully on the broad, striped coconut leaves in some past land, heckling the distant hush. Most probably it was two in the night; the more the clouds moulted their moisture, the faster the rains loaded them with sprays. The showers washed away the ink of my old handwritten notes as I held them. I remained rooted at the spot—dare I tread lightly on these ample leaves? Lightning cracked and the sky was awash with light. Such lovely land and sky, how can I walk away? Is life possible beyond them? Yet, this place is not home, it is Zagreb. The wind has grown tipsy from the intermingled scents of ripe apples and vineyards, combining with whiffs strange and familiar. For the first time, I am in love with Zagreb. The showers and the untamed gusts, they must have called on my native land too, must have soaked those also who never bared their heart to me. What terrible helplessness, what crippling restrictions and curbs of modesty!

Still, '*je bhabei tumi sakal dekho surja kintu ektai, jato bhage bhag karo na prem, man tomar ektai*' (howsoever you behold the dawn, the sun is always one; howsoever you split your love, your heart is always one).

Sometimes I laugh at our lives being wasted in indecisions and hesitancy. We are unable to disclose that we yearn for the touch of a special, loving, reassuring hand; he needs only to caress my head tenderly. We waver and the moment slips away. Clouds gather and the skies open up, followed by a spotless, bright, clear sky. Raindrops suspended on boughs and fronds tumble down. I hark back to a bright, cloudless, brilliant Santiniketan dawn when colourful birds foraging for food had whipped up a commotion. They hopped in different directions with a single purpose—to hoard food in the nests to save their chicks from starving during the rains. I set out for the countryside across the railway track with Chaitalidi, an inhabitant of Berhampore and an ardent Sain devotee. Someone had told her about a master tantric; it was big trouble finding his whereabouts.

The fragrance of the incense had cast a mysterious atmosphere in the neat mud and grass hut in a blind alley. Chaitalidi called out to a middle-aged woman in a simple cotton sari, pumping water from a rusty hand pump in the middle of the courtyard, '*Ei Maya Di, keman achho*?' (Hey Mayadi, how are you?). It was my first passing meeting with Mayadi. A prophecy was eventually pronounced in a solemn, resonant voice inside the bolted room in Bangla—Miss Chaitali Ghoshal, daughter of Saugata Ghoshal, would enjoy every material pleasure in life—house, orchards, cars, and money. I shall never forget the glow on Chaitalidi's face. Suddenly, she pulled me by the hand and the tantrik's bloodshot, dazed eyes scrutinised my weak, thin, long palm. In five seconds, I hear the prediction about myself, '*Tumi prem kore khubi duhkha pabe, emni tumi khubi nam korbe*' (You will reap a lot of grief in love but you will be famous). Who does not know that love is followed by heartbreak? But I do not believe the augury. I smile inwardly at the charade. Chaitalidi offers money to him and we return happily to Santiniketan by the red gravel road along the canal, via Shyambati.

Today, as I stand in Turkebana Yelachica, I summon up the image of dark Maya Dasi. Her destiny was exploited by priests in the shadowy colonnades of the Minakshi Temple, to lead the life of a *devdasi* for sixteen years before settling down eventually in Bengal, in the afternoon of life. Mayadi, who had survived the misery of being a *devdasi* and who had been brutalised by the organised crime syndicate of the temples, was quite blunt. When I posed a childish question, 'Why do you sell yourself? Why don't you do something else?' she spat out a reply with a dark, filthy glob of tobacco, '*Thak beshi matha ghamio na, giye nijer kaj samlao*' (Don't worry too much, go mind your own business). Her only possessions were a cracked earthen pot and the hoe blade with the help of which she cooked her food on the earthen oven. Around fifty, with shining black skin, she had every available addiction—be it marijuana or whatever. She easily earned twenty to twenty-five rupees a day from her customers. Her intestines might be boiling from the pangs of hunger but if she laid her hands on *ganja* or *bhang*, she would transfigure into a queen and traipse on cracked soles, brass dancing bells tied to the legs, moving to the tunes of different songs.

Tragically, I did not understand many of her songs although she could have explained them then. Sometimes, a refrain haunts me all day, resonating in *drut vilambit*. She had sung, '*Chokher aloy dekhechhilem chokher bahire / antare aj dekhbo jakhan alok nahi re*' (I have seen the outside world through my eyes; now, when I have lost them, I would seek it within). What sort of a life do women like Maya lead? A life of insects and bugs, sans food, sans home, sans security—a mindless passage from birth to death. Nobody cares for them, not even they themselves. Let alone being offered the dignity of a woman, nobody considers them even human beings. The body becomes a cloak; no fond gaze ever caresses her soul. The body is the concern. An entire life is spent in search of proper respect for the body created from the five elements. A woman who realises that her body is her daily bread, her food, and a roof over her head, finds selling it the most difficult yet the simplest chore. What pain does a woman suffer in trading herself! The body must be bared before others to buy clothes to cover it. She hunts for customers to fill the bellies of the children borne by her body. Enduring spittle, semen, blood, and rising vomit, she offers herself, handling customer after customer. Blast the infernal creature who claims that women turn into prostitutes for the sake of carnal pleasure!

***

I have noted down Imogen's story too in the journal. I had not the smallest hunch that on this bleak, barren, desolate day, my memory of Maya Dasi would bond with the memory of Imogen. The rains have stopped; I have bought some foodstuff and put it in the fridge. I had cooked potato-stuffed *parathas* in the morning but I have lost my appetite. I had also planned to reorganise the journal but instead, I enjoyed walking in the downpour. I have plenty of groceries and a capable wardrobe. The embassy takes good care of me. I have friends, relatives too, yet sometimes I have to throw away the leftovers. Ironically, I find it difficult to write about the women that peddle themselves for pieces of bread. I open the pages written in June. The cuckoo warbles all through June and July in my country, but here, it is hard to spot even an ant. A silence, a hush, a lull, a stillness drapes everything although these are the summers, and we have cast off our coats and sweaters. The sun shines till nine in the evening. It becomes rather hot if the window remains closed. I am wearing my Indian clothes. However, the weather in my heart has taken a turn. My earlier eagerness to talk to my people back home has been replaced by apathy. Sometimes the phone intrudes or else I occupy myself with studies, translations, and this journal of mine containing Imogen and Angelina. I realise they would never read these pages. They would never know that a stranger has documented their experiences and the stillness gripping their souls in the Devanagari script.

***

I will speak about Imogen first. On a bleak, interminable afternoon, with starvation staring her in face, she decided to contact the traffickers, deserting her parents, her small brother, and her lover, Porsha. She had no idea that her neighbour who was arranging her illegal migration by tempting her with a waitress's job, was actually conning her. She did not listen to Porsha, 'Don't leave Imogen. We will manage somehow, we can catch fish, or work as porters on the dock, I'm sure I'll find something. You won't return if you go'. 'Surely I will', sixteen-year-old Imogen whispered, sinking in his arms, almost breaking into sobs. They had played hide and seek in the rocks, made sand castles, strung tiny oyster shells into garlands, and counted the lights of the ships at night on the shore. Will they ever relive the serenity? 'They have assured me a job, they say you can earn plenty in Italy if you work even half a day.' She struggled to convince her boyfriend like a mature woman, two years her senior. 'No, don't leave, be with me, close to my heart; let me gaze at your face till eternity. Better times will come. Martha will let me have the boat after the death of my stepfather—don't leave. I will miss caressing your tresses, your angelic smile. They are my treasures. We can marry in two years. You will sing to my tunes, Imogen! I'll play my harmonica for none but you.' The sobs choked. But how could Imogen stay back? Her resolve grew stronger every time she looked at her small, perpetually hungry brother. Had she listened to him, she would not have suffered this accursed fate.

She was brought to Arizona Market in 1999—since then, eleven long years have passed but she has not left. How will she return? Is Porsha still waiting? No! Someone from her village had informed her that he was now the proud father of two kids. Twins, chubby, cuddly, charming kids—Imogen might have been their mother. Porsha used to tell her that their son would look like her, and the daughter, like him. Porsha must be catching fish, his wife would be watching from the door, waiting for him—their life surging in tantrums and love, fondness and passion. He must have forgotten her. The door never opens if a woman wants to return. Does she not yearn for Porsha? Imogen chuckles a hollow, false laugh, her tongue whispers a 'no' but the eyes belie—I want to be the same old Imogen again! How intensely did we bond! Do you remember Porsha, once you bought fruit juice with the coins I had saved! Are you still the same, pure Porsha? I don't want a dark shadow to rob your innocence. Would you know me if you saw me? This chasm of eleven years—a period that showered dollars on me but took away the dignity of life, delivered food but snatched away my hunger, offered a bed but robbed my sleep! Why didn't you save me? You had pledged to marry me! You must have forgotten me. The passage from our village to this place was quick but the way back is interminable.

Imogen has been sending her hard-earned money to her parents for the last eight years. Sandy shards of sadness lacerate her eyes but she hides them behind layers of blue and green eyeliners. 'You can leave now, Imogen—take up some other job.' Her face hardens. Evidently, either she is not willing to return, or else, all roads leading home are barred. Imogen's story of her eleven years is terrible. Police beatings, detention centres, terrible customers, brawls with pimps, the occasional sympathy, and the equations of avarice and temptations. I have seen her—she is a strapping woman, a tall and robust mistress—three girls work for her. She offers them protection and care. Imogen says they respect her—it is ironical to hear the word 'respect' in this profession. She uses the power of money and her charms to deal with the police. I discovered her through an NGO that sends doctors to Arizona Market every week. A glance at her stony face makes one suspect if emotions survive in any nook of her heart. Her room is stuffed with all sorts of goodies; obviously, her parents must have waded out of their poverty now. The harmonica crooning in the twilight must have drowned in the din of life; nobody back home would realise that blonde Imogen had learnt the ropes of earning Euros competently. She has contracted a couple of illnesses—the doctor has warned her to quit. It has been years since Imogen lost the sense of distinguishing between night and day—she sleeps in snatches when there are no customers. I want to ask her, 'Do you ever catch the faraway melody of the harmonica? Does your heart ache for him?' Dreams and memory, too, are a luxury enjoyed over a full belly. Alas, had she listened to Porsha's call, she would not have led this dismal life then. What if she returns? She replies nonchalantly, 'What for?' The entire village would learn that Imogen is a hooker, not a waitress. She sometimes calls home but never dreams of going back.

***

Imogen had requested me to withhold her real name. I respect her wish. However, I am really inquisitive about the country's police system. Maybe the riddle will be solved in August. The sun beats harshly in July here but sometimes showers make the day nippy. Classes will resume at the university in September so I must finish my search before the session begins. I have tried to speak to many people, but it is hard to say why they evade the issue that has impacted a major part of this East European region. Most of them shrug. Girls and women are still trafficked to Western Europe. I come across such accounts in libraries, based on police records and newspaper reports. It is certain that Croatia is the portal for sex trafficking in Western Europe. Girls and women from Slovenia, Bosnia, and Serbia are transported here without any difficulty. After the war, large troops of the international armies stayed back in the area, which helped build up a favourable climate for sex work despite efforts to check it. The National Counter-Trafficking Body and Gender Equality Commission took a number of corrective measures, but neither trafficking nor sex work could be held down.

***

These are confusing times. Occasionally, I am convinced that ignorance is bliss. Nobody had told me about the dark secrets of this land when I had departed India. People who had visited different European countries as visiting professors through the Indian Council for Cultural Relations Programme, had only admiration for Europe. One friend had advised me to take up a slew of tours to keep loneliness at bay. Another told me that we are not merely teachers but also cultural ambassadors of our nation. A friend reported that one teacher on the job rang up home every day, sniffling that someone should join him to chase away his loneliness. Some even offered lessons on how to take care of oneself. I don't think these opinions and advice assisted me in any way. We learn only from our own experiences. However, my interest in the things and happenings here is mounting. Ivan, Sergei, and Doctor Tomislav Meretic have helped multiply the curiosity.

***

I am travelling to Sarajevo by train. Guldane has turned down my request to accompany me. I do not have much luggage. The track, flanked by greenery, runs between hills. The houses are not tall but they are large and look durable. There are stuccoed buildings. I was warned about stringent passport checks. The train from Zagreb reaches Sarajevo at four o'clock. The 288 kilometre journey has taken around six hours. No bedding was available on the train so I was unable to sleep. Sarajevo does not have an Indian embassy. The Indian mission in Budapest looks after the issues in Bosnia-Herzegovina. India's relations with Bosnia are cordial because Marshal Tito was a good friend of Jawaharlal Nehru. I am staying at City Hotel—it is clean, cosmopolitan, and carries an Indian ambience. I can see the fusion of the cultures of Turkey, Serbia, and Croatia in this cosmopolitan city. Muslims are in a majority. I am going to Begova Dzamija, the biggest mosque here.

Constructed in 1531, a fine example of Islamic architecture, it is orderly and stolid. The entrance of every house in the residential part behind the mosque is adorned with flowers, mostly creepers. The streets run up and down as if on a hill, with the houses nestling close to each other. Bolkovec has rented one of the houses. I have already called her, she can talk in English. It is a common-looking building; it appears she is a pensioner. Around fifty-five, she must have been a robust woman in her youth. She has put on a long skirt and her hair is in two brown braids. Her oblong, largish face remains aloof in the first meeting but grows tender gradually. Folks here are quite formal initially, but over the course of time, they soften. She serves me *nasa* coffee—it is also called Turkish coffee. The coffee has been served with proper etiquette, the cups bear exquisite patterns. On my way here, I saw artisans embellishing pots and decorative pieces. There is a surprising amount of interest in arts and aesthetics in this town of bullets and massacres—humans never really tire or accept defeat. Flowers buried in ashes survive the apocalypse. People beautify their abodes with flowers. Hope sustains them even after thousands of defeats. In spite of the tears and the suffering, hope never ceases to exist. The will to survive is the supreme reality. Death, the departure of close ones, cheating, deceit, and lies—humans overcome everything. The happy memories of the past keep hope alive.

Dolac Market is bustling. Hundreds of kiosks are selling fruit and vegetables. Who can imagine that the bazaar, filled with glittering lights and fair, pink faces covered in scarves, is the spot where sixty-five innocent civilians lost their lives in the bombing by Serbian Chetniks in 1995? The war ravaged not only the hearts and the minds of the people but also these sturdy edifices. Walking by Sarajevo station, I could see the marks of the bullets even after a gap of fifteen-odd years. Are human beings really so resilient? Bozac used to tell me, 'You won't understand the shock of when I saw the corpse of my eight-year-old daughter. Imagine, your own pulsating, throbbing, blood-dripping heart has been placed on a rock and is being pounded ceaselessly; your own blood splatters on you but people advise you casually—let it be, turn your back on everything, live again'. His words were loaded with lethal, numbing iciness—my heart shivered. I remember Bozac vehemently. How desolate must have been his lonely years, hounded by the toxic memories of bloodshed and war! He did not begin afresh; he lost himself in books and in earning money to purchase them. He was not anxious to perpetuate his bloodline, and I don't think he had a friend. He often talked to himself but he was not crazy. His lonesomeness had taught him to search within, to be his own companion. Moreover, what would he have viewed outside himself? Disgruntled, discontented men, cloaked in their venal interests. I don't notice the prettiness and design of the stone buildings in Sarajevo, my eyes hold only the bullet marks on the walls. Sergei Mikhayilic was right when he told me that I never can be a good tourist. I lack the detachment of a sightseer. I am curious about the past and the present but I am too sensitive to study them with indifference. I imagine hands beckoning from the narrow windows of these tall and short structures, calling out frantically for help. My eyes grow moist and blurred with cloudlets of tears.

***

Bolkovec, who was to tell me about Bosnia, especially Arizona Market, had been posted in the capital city Sarajevo in 1998, as the firm Deucromp had recruited several employees for short-term jobs for the UN. Bolkovec has a lot to say and show. The plan is settled. We will start the day after. She will go to the weekly market tomorrow but she has managed to get hold of a sex worker called Angelina.

Angelina does not know how old she is. She has been an independent sex worker for the last five years. She is not really keen on talking to me but there are two people present from the NGO so she answers my questions half-heartedly. She had left a drug de-addiction centre only last month. Long addiction has made her ill. She tried to run away from Arizona Market many times but the flesh-peddlers caught her every time and dragged her back. 'Did the police not help you?' She replies laconically that very few girls seek police assistance. The information about police raids leak beforehand. The girls are instructed on how they are to scatter. They return when the police go away. There are several minor girls in the profession as well, fake birth certificates proliferate.

If a few are caught, they are sent off to the detention centre, which is as dreadful as a prison. A *javna kuca* (brothel) is comparatively paradise. Angelina has no plans to quit. She enjoys a degree of freedom here—she can live as she wants. She has erased the past from her mind or perhaps is not inclined to remember it. I try my best to show her the horrible picture of her insecure future—do you realise that you will have nobody close? Where will you go when you are helpless? Who will be your companion? Do you recollect your home? She is annoyed by the twofold trouble—the first is the problem of translation, and the second is her growing agitation, a withdrawal syndrome. The conversation terminates. I am told that these women receive healthcare and other facilities but they themselves are reluctant to push their way out of addiction. The NGOs too are helpless. They live only as long as they are adrift in their psychotropic world. When the intoxication wears off, they wander in search of new customers to renew their lease of life. Still, there must be at least a few who are disgusted by their profession and are eager to quit. Rees has been working in this sector for the last ten years. He knows that the road to the rehabilitation of sex workers is beset with difficulties. There are several shelter homes where they can lead an honourable life but the sway and web of corruption are pretty dense. Folks in this area very well know how minor girls are coerced into sex work. Psychiatrists say that many of them become mentally ill in old age.

***

I do not fancy hotel food. Since I am a vegan, I have precious few options such as fruit bread and soups. The coffee tastes too bitter. I fondly remember my native fare. Bolkovec realizes my precarious position and escorts me to a bakery. The bread we call *Afghani* is called *pita* here. Another is the tangy, salty bread *lepinja*, made from flour, milk, salt, and baking soda. The *pita* sells twice a week, six in a packet—they are baked in an electric oven with a hot, yeasty aroma. A man wearing gloves bundles them in packets and hands them to the customers. The yeasty black and white bread does not go bad for almost four days. I had planned to enjoy them with jam but the Indian palate craves something spicy. Bolkovec cooks beef for herself and the smell spoils my appetite. Anyway, I have to garner important information from her and verify a few without expressing my discomfort. Bolkovec points out the Olivier salad, also known as Russian salad. It is made with boiled potatoes, mayonnaise, black olive, apple, etc. I tried some in the hotel but it has left an unsavoury taste in my mouth; maybe there was some ham too. My belly is rumbling and I long for mango pickles. I conjure the aroma of stuffed chillies but I have to make do with multigrain bread. It is my private therapy—when I eat something disagreeable, I imagine I am eating the tastiest food on earth or else I finish my meal while watching some foodie channel on TV.

Bolkovec is a divorcee. She was quite reserved in the first meeting but has opened up in the last two days. Gregarious with her interesting anecdotes about Turkey and Bosnia, sometimes she breaks into peals of laughter and sometimes lapses moodily into silence. Her lonely life must have driven her to it, or else it is hard to believe that the vitality of such an intelligent and creative woman, who is working voluntarily in a conflict zone, should appear so dim. Why should I dig into her private life? It is not easy to expose the inner self, almost impossible to understand it. One must descend deep within. Inner journeys are much more complex and demanding than outer ones. Bolkovec has given me a week to go through the reports that she prepared some six years ago.

I marvel at its diligent organisation. She uses an old desktop computer which is covered with a piece of cloth. She is cautious; she has given them to me only to read, not to copy. There is no internet or maybe the modem has been turned off deliberately to prevent me from mailing it. 'You have already submitted the report, why are you so watchful?'

There is no reply. I can hear her loud, melodious voice from the bathroom; evidently, she is in a happy mood. I don't understand the songs despite my best efforts. She comes in with her braided hair in two brown buns. She pulls on a fragrant hookah and the room is filled with a heady scent, overwhelming me. As if the chaste Kalyan raga is playing again. The special guy, who had loved it, used to say that the Kalyan raga inundated him. My heart flutters as if it is the ecstasy of death. Kishori Amonkar emerges from the pen drive and croons, *Laagi lagan more Shyam salone, tum bin kaise beete nis din* (The appointed hour has come, how can I spend my nights and days without you, Oh Shyam!). Bolkovec is oblivious of my presence, humming some local folk song. She describes the musical legacy and traditions of Bosnia and even breaks into songs sometimes. The songs are full of Islam, war, bravery, meetings, and partings. The folk songs have been translated into other European languages by distinguished artistes like Herder, Goethe, and Pushkin. The Islamic influence appears strongly in the more popular *ilahiz* and *quasida*, written in the praise of the almighty Allah. Karlos Santana has concluded in his research that music can alter the molecular structure of the body. When I hear Bolkovec humming, I feel she is neither sad nor defeated but is an aware woman dissipating her heartache with the atoms of music. She does not need any other companion, and she never will.

***

Bolkovec tried to break the spider-web of sex trafficking when she was posted in Sarajevo in 1998. She has noted, 'The moment I started collecting evidence on sex trafficking, skeletons started tumbling out. Many of the UN officials posted in different countries were found to be connected with the trade. As soon as the higher authorities got wind of my investigation, they kicked me out'. Her report reminds me of the report of the former police officer from Philadelphia, David Lamb. He had remarked that prima facie it appeared that several UN employees were involved but he had failed to understand why they were not investigated by the UN (U.N. Halted Probe of Officers' Alleged Role in Sex Trafficking, *The Washington Post,* December 27, 2001). The evidence collected by Lamb also included several testimonies from Bosnian police sources. Since he was part of the system, it was not difficult for him to examine the police records. He documented, in detail, the depositions of the women that had escaped from brothels, reformatories, and detention centres, and some that had returned home.

Bolkovec refers to Lamb's account as an illustration in her report. She cites that an officer visited the Romanian embassy to get work permits for two women and he asked Lamb to order the Bosnian police to stop their investigation into sex trafficking. A secret inquiry report has disclosed that four Romanian officers complained against a Canadian officer named Rosario Loana because he had interrogated a few of the women. I had always thought that only we Indians and Third World citizens are shady and that our sense of morality is much too flexible, but these exclusive European encounters have changed my opinion. Bolkovec brings up the issue of minor girls offered as gifts by the brothel owners to the international peacekeeping forces. Many of the girls identified the officers before the police but no disciplinary action followed. Instead, facetious arguments were offered, for instance, the officers and soldiers had left behind their homes and countries, and if they were sexually starved, the quality of their work would suffer. Newspapers and the media took up the matter strongly because the guilty soldiers had been let off with a slap on the wrist. Bolkovec says that the International Crisis Group launched a special trafficking operations programme in 2000. Its task was to direct the local police forces and rescue women confined as sex slaves. Altogether, 200 raids were conducted by July 2001 with the assistance of the local police.

On 1 August 2002, a special team including the Bosnian police was constituted by the UN. 600 raids were made on restaurants and bars and 182 women smuggled in from Romania, Ukraine, and Moldova were rescued. Seventy-eight bars were allowed operations in spite of their being marked as brothels. According to a May 2002 newspaper report, only seven persons were held guilty of the crime of trafficking. They served sentences ranging from four to thirty months. They also had to deposit sureties of 600 to 1,000 dollars. Bolkovec was unhappy with the government's attitude. She claims that in Bosnia alone there are 6,000 to 10,000 migrant women who have been pushed into this profession. She has extensive statistics to show how they are sold to pimps for 500 to 1,500 dollars after their passports are seized. At certain locations, small girls and women are segregated forcibly and auctioned like heifers. Women with kids go cheap, old women are cut-rate (they are considered fit only for the jobs of guards or maids), virgins and good-looking women are prized. They have to undergo a crude, brutal, virginity test. Their genitals are examined with metal forceps or fingers. Their teeth and gums are inspected; the test for the belly and back skin is pinching. Prices are fixed accordingly. Pregnant women are millstones. Most often they are forced to undergo abortion before the bidding. Bolkovec's face turns ashen when she describes Arizona Market. I grow anxious. The azan from the mosque is echoing on the horizon, '*Allahu Akbar, ashhadu alla ilaha illallah, ashhadu alla ilaha illallah, ashhadu anna muhammadarrasulullah.*' Most probably it is the evening namaz, I should return to my hotel. I take leave of Bolkovec with a promise to come back tomorrow.

***

Sarajevo converts into a city of lights at night. While returning, I see the rolling hills, the houses that appeared dilapidated during the daylight hours seem to have transformed by the magic wand of the night glow. They look crisp and clean, awash in the cerulean-pink radiance. There is a famous nightclub—lights blink, and the neon sign above announces 'Pussy Cat'. This celebrated nightclub has a chain throughout Eastern Europe. Two bouncers stand guard outside and two girls in striking dresses tempt the passers-by in. There is no entry fee. The food joints remain open till late at night. There is a small chill in the weather. I want to sleep early as I have to visit Bolkovec in the morning.

It is 15 August 2010. Fortunately, I am not in Zagreb. The lavish manner in which our national festivals are celebrated in our embassies makes us forget that India is still a developing country grappling with the challenging issues of food and water. There are generous expenses on wines and delicacies at the parties; many of the guests come only to enjoy Indian food. Yet, the ostentation and artificiality that I have left behind in India is not visible here. In the eastern countries, the image of India is one of delicious dishes, inexpensive tourist spots and hotels, and easy visas. But they also realise that it is an unsafe country for women. Bolkovec's friends Dariza and Miriam went to India once. Their unsavoury experience fills me with shame. It was 2009—they shopped themselves weary, toured the length and breadth of the country, and came to Jammu where they stayed in a hotel. Everything was fine during the day but the hotel owner's son accosted them at night. They refused to open the door despite his persistent knocking. Their passports had already been collected at the reception counter.

It was a gloomy night. In the morning, when the hotel owner returned, the girls felt reassured and checked out of the hotel immediately. They travelled to Delhi because someone had recommended Sadar Bazaar. The two were mobbed; someone pinched them on the buttocks, some others pushed themselves against them. It was with a great deal of difficulty that they exited the narrow streets and returned to their hotel. What plea do I have? It is a common experience for Indian women also, in public places. Miriam's complaint has substance when she says that she is diabetic but that there are no toilets for women in public places or by the roads in India. She also felt bad that men relieved themselves openly, by trees, roads, and cars, while the police looked the other way. However, they savour Indian *parathas*. I invite them to Zagreb—they gift me an embroidery piece and a marble statuette in return.

***

Bolkovec wants to hear what I write. Of all the people I have met so far, she is the only one to offer information without hesitation. Yet, an uneasy silence stretches between us sometimes. She knows several European languages. She has compensated for her years of loneliness by learning the tongues. Today she is dolled up; the hookah carries an azure perfume of tobacco. She tells me about America's dubious role, how it developed Arizona Market into a free trade zone. She gives me statistics on rehabilitation, which is the only ray of hope. Since 1999, 429 women have been reintegrated. Many of these girls, abducted and coerced into prostitution, were hardly twelve to fifteen years old. Foreign soldiers as well as the NATO and UN officials were their customers. People had little left with them when the civil war ended in 1992. There was widespread devastation. The NATO regiments, consisting of 20,000 soldiers, workers, and officials from forty-eight countries associated with the peacekeeping forces, constituted 80 per cent of their clients. It was a lucrative, prospering business. Some of the factors aiding its growth were tractable laws, smuggling, and ruinous economic conditions. Figures show that one out of eight Muslim-Croat families was above the poverty line, while among Serbs it was one out of twenty-five. Eastern Europe has the largest percentage of unemployment. Jobless youths engaged in drug and arms trafficking earlier shifted to sex trafficking after the war because it involved small investments with large returns. The punishment, too, was trivial. The Dayton Peace Accord provided not only full authority to the UN but also gave free rein to the NATO soldiers to restore peace. They enjoyed the privilege of special courts and were extended diplomatic immunity against any disciplinary action in Bosnia. Bosnia was reduced almost to a colony.

***

Everyone I met through Bolkovec has mentioned this spider-web of war, displacement, and sex trafficking. When I go through the notes I made in the journal last week, the bitter truth mocking government machinery and fundamental rights, surfaces. Capitalism, money, and inequitable distribution of assets, along with dislodgment, encourage trafficking. No country in the world is free from the net of traffickers. In the last few years, it has grown into an industry. The first victims of economic crises and depression are always the women; their demand and supply are dependent on the economic condition of a country. The world over, especially in post-war Europe, European women were used as sex objects with impunity. When they became available, the demand for Asian women diminished. The expenditure on their upkeep and transit was lower and the profit margins were bigger. They were willing to do anything to escape penury. They also met the expectations of European men on the benchmark of complexion and build. Capitalism has turned women into commodities. We must examine how and why the sex market provides them with better wages as compared to many other sectors. It surges during wars or military actions; economic factors and displacement, too, contribute to drawing women to this profession. Often, they accept it as their destiny. They adopt these alternative means of earning due to wars, military actions, the absence of traditional means of earning, and economic and political instability.

The pitiable condition and economic decline of the socialist countries in East Europe also encouraged sex trafficking. An International Organization for Migration report mentions that trafficking is a major issue in regions of former united Yugoslavia even ten years after the war. Around 500,000 women are enmeshed; 120,000 children and women are smuggled into European Union through the Balkans every year. Seventy per cent of the women working in Soho take this route. A talk with the women reveals that sex trafficking is connected with rapes during a war in a major way. The practice of forcing women to sell their bodies after they are brought to the rape camps is a terribly barbaric and heinous act. The British author Roy Gutman has written an article in *News Day* titled 'Shame in Bosnia'. It is about the Kontiki brothel in Sarajevo. Muslim girls are forced into prostitution and sex slavery for the Serbs. Gutman also reported that the UN soldiers were clients of the rape victims, they never extended them safety or security. They were often forced into UN military vehicles and taken to secret destinations.

***

I try to read out portions of my notes to Bolkovec but she retorts, 'Will your countrymen be interested?' How should I respond? Will these journals ever bargain a readership or will they crumble to dust? I don't know. I merely know that no matter which country it is, a woman is the first victim. Bolkovec has asked me to join in for the meal, accompanied by a wine with a lemony aroma. She makes wine from dry fruit at home every year. 'I married twice. There were lovers as well, but none of them gave me real joy. All my husbands and boyfriends stayed for sometime and then left. What I needed, they did not have and what they needed, I didn't have it'. The wine is overpowering her. For the first time, she unlatches the doors of her personal life. A woman, physically and mentally competent, absorbed in her work, can only be a challenge, never a beloved—it is difficult to say why. The more pitiable and innocent she looks, the greater love and attention she receives.

Bolkovec's life has always been a mission. She has undertaken this journey utterly alone although she is esteemed highly in the NGO she is committed to, for alleviating the sex workers' conditions. She has been a member not only of the UN bodies in post-war Bosnia, but of several inquiry committees also, however, it has come to nothing. 'The deeper I dived into the inquiry records, the more upset my colleagues in the UN became. Files containing records of the interviews went missing, I was warned quite a few times with dire threats to drop the investigation. Still, whatever I saw and heard, I emailed it to fifty high-ranking officials with the note, "If you suffer from weak digestion or if you nurture a guilt feeling, avoid looking at it". I was fired after four days.'

Sundry disciplinary actions were taken against a few but she never got back her job again. Since it became hard now to meet the extravagance of the second husband, he divorced her. I congratulate Bolkovec that she has been spared various ignominies. She advises me to interview a couple of women working in Croatia and Italy. I bid farewell to my good friends as I head back to Zagreb.

***

Most of the victims of the Bosnian war never found justice. A few died, some left the country. The display of brute force and sustained hatred against a particular gender manifests itself in heinous acts like rape. Rape and sexual violence are a war strategy. Unless the harshest of punishment is reserved for the perpetrators, no children, women or any other rape victim shall find justice. It is an undeclared national policy in most countries to overlook wartime sexual aggression, in spite of the fact that almost three-fourths of them have signed the Declaration of Commitment to End Sexual Violence in Conflict to stop the savagery.

We went to Lukomir village before returning to Bosnia. It is claimed that it is the highest village in Europe with pristine ways of life. There is no electricity or modern gadgets but people do not feel any discomfort. It is no surprise for me because in India, many villages still don't have electricity. Bolkovec looks tired; the exhaustion under the layers of her make-up is discernible. She held my shoulder all through the tour. Perhaps a person weakens if she reveals everything. Rabindranath Tagore had declared, when he returned to Santiniketan from his last Europe tour, '*Ami oikhane kanthata hariye eshechhi*' (I mislaid my voice there). Now I realise why music eluded him in this phase.

Dr Tomislav Maretic has come to see me in Zagreb. I read out some parts of my Bosnia account to him. He falls silent for long and then offers me the friendly gift of a scarf sent by Mihino in Italy. '*Nemozte pisati ovo. Ne obzaviti ovo*' (Don't write it. Don't publish it.). I nod in the Croatian fashion with a grin. Years have passed on the horns of dilemma—should I publish it or not? The travel journal of the years 2010-11 is liberated finally for a free flight. I regret not listening to my friend. As I revise the pages of the journal, I catch the tune of Rabindranath Tagore's song every dawn:

> *Andhajane deho alo, mritajane deho pran—*
> *Tumi karunamrita sindhu karo karunakana dan.*
> *...Je tomare dake na he tare tumi dako, dako...*
> *Toma hate dure je jay tare tumi rakho rakho.*
>
> (Give light to the sightless, give life to the lifeless / You are an ocean of the nectar of compassion, Give us a few drops of your kindness... / Keep those close too who move away from you.)

I am watching BBC World on TV. The announcement of the draft of the international protocol initiated by William Hague and Angelina Jolie concerning information and investigation of sexual violence is on air,

> 'We appeal to all nations to amend their laws on rape and sexual violence to conform to international standards. We demand for proper training of all soldiers and peacekeeping forces to check sexual violence in the conflict zones. The assaults can be minimised by simple measures like adequate lighting in refugee camps and security escorts with women venturing out to collect firewood. We demand the universal implementation of the basic safety procedures.'

cumin. Years have passed on the horns of dilemma—should I publish it or not? The travel journal of the years 2010-11 is liberated finally for a free flight. I regret not listening to my friend. As I revise the pages of the journal, I search the tune of Rabindranath Tagore song every dawn:

Andhajane deho alo, mritajane deho pran,

tumi karunamrita-sindhu karo karunakana dan.

Shushka hridaya mamo kathin pashana-samo,

prem-salil-dhare sinchaho shushka nayan.

Give light to the sightless, give life to the lifeless / You are an ocean of the nectar of compassion, Give us a few drops of your kindness. / Keep close those too who move away from you...

I am watching BBC World on TV. The announcement of the draft of the international protocol initiated by William Hague and Angelina Jolie concerning information and investigation of sexual violence is on air.

We appeal to all nations to amend their laws on rape and sexual violence to conform to international standards. We demand for proper training of all soldiers and peacekeeping forces to tackle sexual violence in the conflict zones. The survivors can be supported by simple measures like adequate lighting in refugee camps and security escorts while women venturing out to collect firewood. We demand the universal implementation of the best donor practices.

ACKNOWLEDGEMENT

I acknowledge my readers, my students, friends and publishers, especially Ms Meera Jouhri (Rajpal and Sons), Vasundhara (Chhanda Publications) and Somaya Akhtar (Rabon Publications) for taking immense interest in this book and publishing them in different languages. I am grateful to Mr Vikram Nayak for taking deep interest and sharing one of his eminent artworks for the front cover of the book. I am also grateful to Ms Renu K Verma (Vitasta Publications) for publishing the English translation of *Deh hi Desh* (The Body, a Nation). And finally, I am grateful to Prof Rajesh Kumar (Hazaribagh) for taking pains to translate *Deh hi Desh* (The Body, a Nation) into English. Prof Ravi Ranjan (Hyderabad), Dr Raman Sinha (JNU), Dr Manjurani Singh (Santiniketan), Dr Anamika, Dr Praveen Kumar and Sanjay Sahay (Delhi), along with several other friends, deserve my sincerest gratitude.

ABOUT THE AUTHOR

Professor at Centre of Indian Languages, Jawaharlal Nehru University, India, as well as a feminist activist, **Ms. Garima Srivastava** is a renowned literary figure. Her research articles published in scholarly literary and sociology journals are profound intellectual studies in the field. The feminist perspective through which Prof. Garima Srivastava has undertaken to study the condition of women during wars and in post-war periods is a singular inquiry in Hindi literature and language. She has developed a unique theory concerning the dynamics of war all over the world that suggests that it does not matter in which region of the world a war is fought, its eventual agony is borne in the form of indelible physical and mental scars by women.

ABOUT THE TRANSLATOR

Rajesh Kumar is a prominent educationist, translator and author. Formerly Dean, Humanities, at Vinoba Bhave University, Hazaribag, India, he has authored a large number of research articles in several national and international journals. He is on the editorial board of many journals in different disciplines. An ardent environmentalist, he was also secretary of the India chapter of ASLE. His English short stories have been published profusely in India and abroad. Some of the famous works by him are *Incest and Other Poems*, *The Escape and Other Stories*, *The Other Destiny or Pelanty Gobernor*, *The Dalit Face in Indian English Novel*, *Paul Scott and His India*, *English Language Communication Skills: Lab Manual cum Workbook*, *Lords of the Global Village* (Tr.), *The Jungle Within* (Tr.), *Me Borishailla* (Tr.), *Exile* (Tr.), and *The Toxic Tribal Land of Marang Goda* (Tr.). His Hindi poems have been translated into several languages.